# THE
# LIVING
# COMPANY

# THE
# LIVING
# COMPANY

*Arie de Geus*

Foreword by *Peter M. Senge*

HARVARD BUSINESS SCHOOL PRESS
*Boston, Massachusetts*

Nan Stone and Art Kleiner, Editors

The ideas and views expressed in this book are the author's only.

Requests for permission to use or reproduce material from this book
should be directed to permissions@hbsp.harvard.edu, or mailed to
Permissions, Harvard Business School Publishing, 60 Harvard Way,
Boston, Massachusetts 02163.

**Library of Congress Cataloging-in-Publication Data**

De Geus, Arie.
The living company / by Arie de Geus.
p. cm.
Includes index.
ISBN 0-87584-782-X (alk. paper)
1. Industrial management. 2. Corporations—Case studies.
I. Title.
HD31.G438   1997
658—dc21
96-48384
CIP

ISBN 1-57851-820-2 (pbk)
The paper used in this publication meets the requirements of the
American National Standard for Permanence of Paper for
Publications and Documents in Libraries and Archives Z39.48-1992.

# Contents

*Foreword*    Peter M. Senge                                    *vii*
*Acknowledgments*                                               *xiii*
*Prologue: The Lifespan of a Company*                            *I*

## Learning

1    The Shift from Capitalism to a Knowledge Society / 15
2    The Memory of the Future / 22
3    Tools for Foresight / 38
4    Decision Making as a Learning Activity / 55

## Persona (Identity)

5    Only Living Beings Learn / 77
6    Managing for Profit or for Longevity: Is There a Choice? / 100

## Ecology

7    Flocking / 131
8    The Tolerant Company / 142
9    The Corporate Immune System / 159

132185

# Evolution

10    Conservatism in Financing / 171
11    Power: Nobody Should Have Too Much / 187


*Epilogue: The Company of the Future*                      *199*
*Notes*                                                    *203*
*Index*                                                    *209*
*About the Author*                                         *215*

# Foreword

*Peter M. Senge*

IT WAS THROUGH ARIE DE GEUS, WHOM I MET OVER 15 YEARS ago, that I first became seriously acquainted with the concepts of organizational learning. That meeting began the journey of a lifetime.

He introduced me to the famous study done at Royal Dutch/Shell, where he was the coordinator of planning worldwide, which found that the average life expectancy of Fortune 500 firms, from birth to death, was only 40 to 50 years. The study also found many companies over 200 years old. Arie convinced me that most corporations die prematurely—the vast majority before their fiftieth birthday. The majority of large corporations, he said, suffer from learning disabilities. They are somehow unable to adapt and evolve as the world around them changes.

More importantly, he got me thinking for the first time about the connections between low life expectancy and low vitality of firms while they are still operating. Both are symptoms of the overall health of the enterprise. Like individuals who are unhealthy and can expect an early demise, most large, apparently successful corporations are profoundly unhealthy. The members of these organizations do not experience that their company is suffering from low life expectancy. They experience poor corporate health as work stress, endless struggles for power and control, and the cynicism and resignation that result from a work environment that stifles rather than releases human imagination, energy, and commitment. The day-to-day climate of most organizations is probably more toxic than we care to admit, whether or not these companies are in the midst of obvious decline.

This is a book of practical philosophy. It has been my experience that extraordinary practitioners like Arie can make unique contributions to management thinking, but that their contributions are rarely acknowledged. Unlike academics who write about what they have thought, practitioners think about what they have lived through. Because the source of their thinking is experience rather than concepts, they show how sometimes the most profound ideas are the simplest.

At the heart of this book is a simple question with sweeping implications: What if we thought about a company as a living being?

This raises the obvious question: What is the alternative view of a company if we do *not* see it as a living being? The alternative view is to see a company as a machine for making money.

The contrast between these two views—machine for making money versus living being—illuminates a host of core assumptions about management and organizations.

I believe that almost all of us adopt the machine assumption without ever thinking about it. In so doing, we probably mold the destiny of individual organizations far more than we imagine.

For example, a machine is owned by someone. We are used to thinking of companies in exactly that way: they are *owned* by owners, usually distinct from the company's members. But what does it mean to say that a living being is owned by someone? Most people in the world would regard the idea that one person owns another as fundamentally immoral. Is it no less problematic with regard to a company?

A machine exists for a purpose conceived of by its builders. Again, this is the conventional view of a company: its purpose is to make as much money as possible for its owners. But living beings have their own purpose. This inherent purpose can never be completely supplanted by the goals of another, even though a living being might respond to others' goals. What happens to the life energy of a living being when it is unable to pursue its purpose?

To be effective, a machine must be controllable by its operators. This, of course, is the overarching *raison d'être* of management—to control the enterprise. But living beings are not controllable in the ways that a machine is. (Anyone doubting this premise might consider their success in controlling their teenagers.) They are "influenceable," but only through complex interactive processes which are just as likely to alter the influencer as the influencee. Are struggles over control not the root of most corporate politics and game playing?

Going further, seeing a company as a machine implies that it is created by someone outside. This is precisely the way most people see corporate systems and procedures—as something created by management and imposed on the organization. Seeing a company as a living being implies that it *creates its own processes,* just as the human body manufactures its own cells, which in turn compose its own organs and bodily systems. Is this not exactly how the informal organization of any large company comes into being? The networks of relationships and communication channels essential to anyone doing any job are indeed created by the people themselves.

Seeing a company as a machine implies that it is fixed, static. It can change only if *somebody* changes it. Seeing a company as a living being means that it evolves naturally.

Seeing a company as a machine implies that its only sense of identity is that given to it by its builders. Seeing a company as a living being means that it has its own sense of identity, its own personhood.

Seeing a company as a machine implies that its actions are actually reactions to goals and decisions made by management. Seeing a company as a living being means that it has its own goals and its own capacity for autonomous action.

Seeing a company as a machine implies that it will run down, unless it is rebuilt by management. Seeing a company as a living being means that it is capable of regenerating itself, of continuity as an identifiable entity beyond its present members.

Seeing a company as a machine implies that its members are employees or, worse, "human resources," humans standing in reserve, waiting to be used. Seeing a company as a living being leads to seeing its members as human work communities.

Finally, seeing a company as a machine implies that it learns only as the sum of the learning of its individual employees. Seeing a company as a living being means that it can learn as an entity, just as a theater troop, jazz ensemble, or championship sports team can actually learn as an entity. In this book, Arie argues that *only* living beings can learn.

It is hard for me to ponder the above list of characteristics of machines versus living beings and not feel drawn to the view that Arie puts forward. Why, then, I wonder, have I not come to this view earlier? Why does it seem so difficult for me to *actually* think of a company as a living being? Why does this very simple idea seem not so very easy to internalize?

Is it that we think life starts and ends with us? Surely, simpler organisms are alive. Why, then, can't we regard more complex organisms, like families or societies or companies, as being alive as well? Is the tide pool, a teeming community of life, any less alive than the anemones, mussels, or hermit crabs that populate it? Is it that our mental model of "company" is just so fixed in our minds that we cannot suspend it? Or are we simply not willing to suspend it? If, indeed, we have thought of the companies of which we have been a part as machines, this implies that we are mechanical elements in the machine. A machine does not have living parts. For many of us, this has undoubtedly fostered a deep antipathy toward our organizations. At some level, we deeply resent being made machinelike, in order to fit into the machine. If there is some element of truth to this, it probably says a lot about just how important Arie's simple question actually is.

As Arie points out, the machine metaphor is so powerful that it shapes the character of most organizations. They become more like machines than like living beings because their members *think* of them that way.

So, perhaps our first mandate is to shift our thinking. As Einstein said, "Problems cannot be solved at the same level of awareness that created them." As we do this, the host of practical insights Arie offers for how a company as a living being might plan, learn, and manage and govern itself will prove invaluable steppingstones into what for most of us will be a very different world.

It might also help to reflect that, as odd as Arie's view might at first seem to some of us, it is in fact quite old. Apparently cultures around the world have embraced similar notions for a very long time. In Swedish, the oldest term for "business" is *nårings liv,* literally "nourishment for life." The ancient Chinese characters for "business," at least 3,000 years old, are

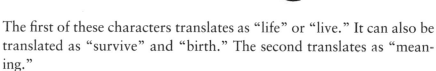

The first of these characters translates as "life" or "live." It can also be translated as "survive" and "birth." The second translates as "meaning."

As we enter the twenty-first century, it is timely, perhaps even critical, that we recall what human beings have understood for a very long time—that working together can indeed be a deep source of life meaning. Anything less is just a job.

Peter M. Senge
December 6, 1996

# Acknowledgments

THE MATERIAL FOR THIS BOOK HAS ACCUMULATED OVER MANY years in a constant dialogue with many people. It was an integral part of my being together with colleagues at Shell, who came from many countries and from varied backgrounds and with whom I worked in the demanding milieu of a multinational company. It was also conducted with the many people I met in the world of international business. And perhaps most important, it was an intense, indispensable element of my work with Group Planning colleagues, many of whom are mentioned by name in this book for their specific contributions to the body of thought on the living, learning company. And around Shell Group Planning there was and is that network of remarkable people from musicians and film directors to academics and consultants that provided such inspiration.

All together, these people supplied me with the material of which experience is made. Together we lived through the events that have become the growth buds for questions about companies—their purpose, their very nature, and what that means for their managers. The questions led to a search for answers, and it is this search that forms the backbone of the book. In the first month of my first year at university, the professor of philosophy looked sternly at us novices and said, "Remember, you will never have an original thought in your life. Every thought, every idea will already have been thought long ago by someone else." He was right. I owe a great debt to all my interlocutors in that dialogue.

The writing of this book would never have occurred were it not for Harriet Rubin, a graduate in poetry and a publisher with sharp intuition, who realized there could be a book long before anyone else, with the exception of Napier Collyns. Over the years, both never ceased to encourage me finally to write that book. Still, it took Nan Stone, then a senior editor at the *Harvard Business Review,* a week of her annual leave to coach me through the material and to help me arrive at the conclusion that, after all, it might be worth a try. Her prompting and my growing experience of lecturing in many countries for a wide range of audiences finally crystallized and honed the ideas that had germinated in the rich environment of Shell's planning coordination.

Those ideas in manuscript form received the attention of an additional coach, Marjorie Williams of the Harvard Business School Press, whose editorial suggestions led to further development of the book. Napier Collyns and Nan Stone persuaded Art Kleiner, historian and author, to take the time to reshape the manuscript around its main theme of "the living company." My thanks go to all for entering into the dialogue.

# Prologue

# The Lifespan of a Company

IN THE WORLD OF INSTITUTIONS, COMMERCIAL CORPORATIONS
are newcomers. Their history comprises only 500 years of activity in
the Western world, a tiny fraction of the time span of human civilization. In that time, as producers of material wealth, they have had immense success. They have been the major vehicle for sustaining the ex-
ploding world population with goods and services that make civilized
life possible. In the years ahead, as developing countries expand their
standards of living, corporations will be more needed than ever.

Yet, if you look at them in the light of their potential, most commercial corporations are dramatic failures—or, at best, underachiev-
ers. They exist at a primitive stage of evolution; they develop and exploit only a fraction of their potential. For proof, you need only
consider their high mortality rate. The average life expectancy of a
multinational corporation—Fortune 500 or its equivalent—is between
40 and 50 years. This figure is based on most surveys of corporate
births and deaths. A full one-third of the companies listed in the 1970
Fortune 500, for instance, had vanished by 1983—acquired, merged,
or broken to pieces.[1] Human beings have learned to survive, on average, for 75 years or more, but there are very few companies that are
that old and flourishing.

There *are* a few. The Stora company, for example, is a major paper, pulp, and chemical manufacturer; it has had the character of a publicly owned company from its very early beginnings, more than 700 years ago, as a copper mine in central Sweden. The Sumitomo Group has its origins in a copper casting shop founded by Riemon Soga in the year 1590. Examples like these are enough to suggest that the *natural* average lifespan of a corporation should be as long as two or three centuries.

I didn't see these astonishing statistics until I had already spent more than two decades as a professional manager. It took another decade for their implications to fully sink in. I worked all my life for a major Anglo-Dutch multinational, the Royal Dutch/Shell Group of companies. Born and educated in Holland, I went to work for Shell directly out of college. I held jobs ranging from accountant to group planning coordinator (coordinator is the group's equivalent of a senior vice president), working on three continents and in Shell operating companies whose businesses ranged from refining to marketing to exploration and from oil to chemicals to metals. As it happens, I am a second-generation Shell man, because my father worked for the same company. During our two generations, he and I clocked 64 working years. So it cannot be a great surprise that, for a long time, I took it for granted that most companies (including Royal Dutch/Shell) simply could not die. They would naturally exist forever.

Well, they don't. Even the big, solid companies, the pillars of the society we live in, seem to hold out for not much longer than an average of 40 years. And that 40-year figure, short though it seems, represents the life expectancy of companies of a considerable size. These companies have already survived their first 10 years, a period of high corporate "infant mortality." In some countries, 40 percent of all newly created companies last less than 10 years. A recent study by Ellen de Rooij of the Stratix Group in Amsterdam indicates that the average life expectancy of all firms, regardless of size, measured in Japan and much of Europe, is only 12.5 years.[2] I know of no reason to believe that the situation in the United States is materially better.

The implications of these statistics are depressing. Between the centuries of age of a Stora or a Sumitomo and the average lifespan— whether 12.5 or 40 years—there exists a gap which represents the wasted potential in otherwise-successful companies. The damage is not merely a matter of shifts in the Fortune 500 roster; work lives, communities, and economies are all affected, even devastated, by premature corporate deaths. Moreover, there is something unnatural in the high corporate mortality rate; no living species, for instance, endures such a large gap between its maximum life expectancy and its average realization. Moreover, few other types of institutions—churches, armies, or universities—seem to have the abysmal demographics of the corporate life form.

Why, then, do so many companies die prematurely? There are many speculations about the reason, and this area undoubtedly needs much more research. However, there is accumulating evidence that corporations fail because the prevailing thinking and language of management are too narrowly based on the prevailing thinking and language of economics. To put it another way: Companies die because their managers focus on the economic activity of producing goods and services, and they forget that their organizations' true nature is that of a community of humans. The legal establishment, business educators, and the financial community all join them in this mistake.

## Some Companies Last Hundreds of Years

These understandings stemmed from a surprising study which we conducted in 1983, when I was coordinator of planning for the Royal Dutch/Shell Group. Royal Dutch/Shell, based in Britain and the Netherlands, is one of the top three corporations in the world in size—composed internally of more than 300 companies in more than 100 countries around the world. All of these companies are co-owned by an interlinked pair of holding companies, one Dutch and one British. The history of the Shell Group dates back to the 1890s. Its British founders began as sellers of oil for the lamps of the Far East (Shell was named after the fact that seashells were used as money in the Far East), while the Dutch founders imported kerosene from Sumatra. From the moment they merged, in 1906, Shell's primary business was the worldwide production and marketing of oil and petroleum.

That was true at least until the 1970s. Then, feeling the pressure of the energy crisis, Shell's managers (along with managers of other oil companies and firms in other industries) were swept up in the trend of diversification. We entered into metals, nuclear power, and other businesses that were new to us, with varying degrees of success. By the early 1980s, serious doubts had surfaced in the Shell Group about the wisdom of this diversification. Yet we weren't sure we could survive with our core oil and petroleum business alone. Reserves of reasonably accessible oil were projected to last three or four decades before they would be exhausted. Shell executives cannot avoid discussing the question: Is there life after oil? What other businesses might Shell reasonably enter? How might we prepare for switching to them as our primary business? And what effect would that switch have on our company as a whole?

In the early 1980s, the planners in my department conducted some research to see what other companies were doing with their business portfolios. But Lo van Wachem, then chairman of the Committee of Managing Directors (the most senior board of Royal Dutch/Shell managers) pointed out that the companies we had studied were nowhere near the size of the Shell Group. Size, when you get to the level of turning over $100 billion per year, presents its own unique problems. The examples were also too recent. Other companies' diversification moves had not yet stood the test of time. Some of Shell's diversification moves, like the opening of the chemicals business, were already at least 30 years old, and we *still* didn't have consensus within the company about their value.

Van Wachem would be more interested, he added, if the planners could show him some examples of large companies that were older than Shell and relatively as important in their industry. Most importantly, he wanted to know about companies that, during their history, had successfully weathered some fundamental change in the world around them—such that they still existed today with their corporate identity intact.

That was an interesting question. Looking for companies older than Shell would mean going back to the final quarter of the nineteenth century—or earlier, into the first years of the Industrial Revolution.

Tens of thousands of companies had existed in those days, in every corner of the world. But which ones were still alive today with their corporate identity intact?

Some companies exist only as a name, a brand, an office building, or a memory: remnants of a glorious past. But after some research and reflection, we began building up a list of companies that met van Wachem's criteria. In North America, there were DuPont, the Hudson Bay Company, W. R. Grace, and Kodak—all older than Shell. A handful of Japanese companies traced their origins to the seventeenth and eighteenth centuries and were still thriving. They included Mitsui, Sumitomo, and the department store Daimaru. Mitsubishi and Suzuki were younger; they traced their origins merely to the nineteenth century, having emerged from the business opportunities that opened up around the Meiji Restoration (1868). During that period of fundamental change in Japan, sparked by Admiral Perry's first visit of 1853, some ancient Japanese companies had gotten into serious difficulties; but Mitsui, Sumitomo, and Daimaru had survived with their corporate identities intact.

In present-day Europe, a sizable number of firms were 200 or more years old. In fact, there were so many such firms in the United Kingdom that they had their own trade association, the Tercentenarians Club, which only accepts member companies over 300 years old. However, most of these were family firms that did not meet our size requirements; many of them still under the control of the founding family dynasty.

We commissioned the study, written by two Shell planners and two outside business school professors, to examine the question of corporate longevity. From the very first moment, we were startled by the small number of companies that met van Wachem's criteria of being large and older than Shell. In the end, we found only 40 corporations, of which we studied 27 in detail, relying on published case histories and academic reports. We wanted to find out whether these companies had something in common that could explain why they were such successful survivors.

After all of our detective work, we found four key factors in common:

1. Long-lived companies were sensitive to their environment. Whether they had built their fortunes on knowledge (such as DuPont's technological innovations) or on natural resources (such as the Hudson Bay Company's access to the furs of Canadian forests), they remained in harmony with the world around them. As wars, depressions, technologies, and political changes surged and ebbed around them, they always seemed to excel at keeping their feelers out, tuned to whatever was going on around them. They did this, it seemed, despite the fact that in the past there were little data available, let alone the communications facilities to give them a global view of the business environment. They sometimes had to rely for information on packets carried over vast distances by portage and ship. Moreover, societal considerations were rarely given prominence in the deliberations of company boards. Yet they managed to react in timely fashion to the conditions of society around them.

2. Long-lived companies were cohesive, with a strong sense of identity. No matter how widely diversified they were, their employees (and even their suppliers, at times) felt they were all part of one entity. One company, Unilever, saw itself as a fleet of ships, each ship independent, yet the whole fleet stronger than the sum of its parts. This sense of belonging to an organization and being able to identify with its achievements can easily be dismissed as a "soft" or abstract feature of change. But case histories repeatedly showed that strong employee links were essential for survival amid change. This cohesion around the idea of "community" meant that managers were typically chosen for advancement from within; they succeeded through the generational flow of members and considered themselves stewards of the longstanding enterprise. Each management generation was only a link in a long chain. Except during conditions of crisis, the management's top priority and concern was the health of the institution as a whole.

3. Long-lived companies were tolerant. At first, when we wrote our Shell report, we called this point "decentralization."

Long-lived companies, as we pointed out, generally avoided exercising any centralized control over attempts to diversify the company. Later, when I considered our research again, I realized that seventeenth-, eighteenth-, and nineteenth-century managers would never have used the word *decentralized*; it was a twentieth-century invention. In what terms, then, would they have thought about their own company policies? As I studied the histories, I kept returning to the idea of "tolerance." These companies were particularly tolerant of activities on the margin: outliers, experiments, and eccentricities within the boundaries of the cohesive firm, which kept stretching their understanding of possibilities.

4. Long-lived companies were conservative in financing. They were frugal and did not risk their capital gratuitously. They understood the meaning of money in an old-fashioned way; they knew the usefulness of having spare cash in the kitty. Having money in hand gave them flexibility and independence of action. They could pursue options that their competitors could not. They could grasp opportunities without first having to convince third-party financiers of their attractiveness.

It did not take us long to notice the factors that did *not* appear on the list. The ability to return investment to shareholders seemed to have nothing to do with longevity. The profitability of a company was a *symptom* of corporate health, but not a *predictor* or *determinant* of corporate health. Certainly, a manager in a long-lived company needed all the accounting figures that he or she could lay hands on. But those companies seemed to recognize that figures, even when accurate, describe the past. They do not indicate the underlying conditions that will lead to deteriorating health in the future. The financial reports at General Motors, Philips Electronics, and IBM during the mid-1970s gave no clue of the trouble that lay in store for those companies within a decade. Once the problems cropped up on the balance sheet, it was too late to prevent the trouble.

Nor did longevity seem to have anything to do with a company's material assets, its particular industry or product line, or its country of origin. Indeed, the 40- to 50-year life expectancy seems to be equally valid in countries as wide apart as the United States, Europe, and Japan, and in industries ranging from manufacturing to retailing to financial services to agriculture to energy.

At the time, we chose not to make the Shell study available to the general public, and it still remains unpublished today. The reasons had to do with the lack of scientific reliability for our conclusions. Our sample of 30 companies was too small. Our documentation was not always complete. And, as the management thinker Russell Ackoff once pointed out to me, our four key factors represented a statistical correlation; our results should therefore be treated with suspicion. Finally, as the authors of the study noted in their introduction, "Analysis, so far completed, raises considerable doubts about whether it is realistic to expect business history to give much guidance for business futures, given the extent of business environmental changes which have occurred during the present century."[3]

Nonetheless, our conclusions have recently received corroboration from a source with a great deal of academic respectability. Between 1988 and 1994, Stanford University professors James Collins and Jerry Porras asked 700 chief executives of U.S. companies—large and small, private and public, industrial and service—to name the firms they most admired. From the responses, they culled a list of 18 "visionary" companies. They didn't set out to find long-lived companies, but, as it happened, most of the firms that the CEOs chose had existed for 60 years or longer. (The only exceptions were Sony and Wal-Mart.) Collins and Porras paired these companies up with key competitors (Ford with General Motors, Procter & Gamble with Colgate, Motorola with Zenith) and began to look at the differences. The visionary companies put a lower priority on maximizing shareholder wealth or profits. Just as we had discovered, Collins and Porras found that their most-admired companies combined sensitivity to their environment with a strong sense of identity: "Visionary companies display a powerful drive for progress that enables them to change and adapt without compromising their cherished core ideals."[4]

At Shell, we never conducted any study of similar diligence. Nonetheless, the Shell study remained uppermost in my mind for years. In our unscientific way, we had found four characteristics that seemed, when put together, to give us a description of a highly successful type of company—a company that could survive for very long periods in an ever-changing world, because its managers were good at the management of change.

## Defining the Living Company

Over time, the same four factors that we developed in our study of long-lived companies at Shell have continued to resonate in my mind. Gradually, they began to change my thinking about the real nature of companies—and of what it means for the way that we, managers at all levels, run those companies. I now see these four components this way:

1. *Sensitivity to the environment* represents a company's ability to learn and adapt.
2. *Cohesion and identity,* it is now clear, are aspects of a company's innate ability to build a community and a persona for itself.
3. *Tolerance* and its corollary, *decentralization,* are both symptoms of a company's awareness of ecology: its ability to build constructive relationships with other entities, within and outside itself.
4. And I now think of *conservative financing* as one element in a very critical corporate attribute: the ability to govern its own growth and evolution effectively.

Moreover, the question remains: Why would these same characteristics occur again and again in companies that had managed to outlive others?

In a sense, I have been intrigued by these issues all of my working life, beginning with my time at university. I am convinced that the four characteristics of a long-lived company are not answers. They represent the start of a fundamental inquiry about the nature and success of commercial organizations and their role in the human community.

Not coincidentally, these four basic components have also provided the framework for this book. Put together, they give clues to the real nature of companies, and they form a set of organizing principles of managerial behavior—critical aspects of the work of any manager who wants his or her company to survive and thrive for the long term.

The Shell study also reinforced a concept I have developed since my student days: to consider and talk about a company as a living entity. In this, I do not stand alone. Many people naturally think and speak about a company as if they were speaking about an organic, living creature with a mind and character of its own. This common use of the language is not surprising. All companies exhibit the behavior and certain characteristics of living entities. All companies learn. All companies, whether explicitly or not, have an identity that determines their coherence. All companies build relationships with other entities, and all companies grow and develop until they die. To manage a "living company" is to manage with more or less consistent, more or less explicit appreciation for these facts of corporate life, instead of ignoring them.

It probably doesn't matter very much whether a company is actually *alive* in a strict biological sense, or whether "the living company" is simply a useful metaphor. As we will see throughout this book, to regard a company as a living entity is a first step toward increasing its life expectancy.

This book is about the idea of the living company, its philosophical underpinnings, its application in practice, and the power and capability that seem to come from adopting it.

For the idea of a living company isn't just a semantic or academic issue. It has enormous practical, day-to-day implications for managers. It means that, in a world that changes massively, many times, during the course of your career, you need to involve people in the continued development of the company. The amount that people care, trust, and engage themselves at work has not only a direct effect on the bottom line, but the most direct effect, of any factor, on your company's expected lifespan. The fact that many managers ignore this imperative is one of the great tragedies of our times.

What, then, does managing a living company mean on a day-to-day basis? The path to the answer starts with another question, the question of corporate purpose: What are corporations *for*?

Financial analysts, shareholders, and many executives tell us that corporations exist primarily to provide a financial return. Some economists offer a somewhat broader sense of purpose. Companies, they say, exist to provide products and services, and therefore to make human life more comfortable and desirable. "Customer orientation" and other management fashions have translated this imperative into the idea that corporations exist to serve customers. Politicians, meanwhile, seem to believe that corporations exist to provide for the public good: to create jobs and ensure a stable economic platform for all the "stakeholders" of society.

But, from the point of view of the organization itself—the point of view that allows organizations to survive and thrive—all of these purposes are secondary.

*Like all organisms, the living company exists primarily for its own survival and improvement: to fulfill its potential and to become as great as it can be.* It does not exist solely to provide customers with goods, or to return investment to shareholders, any more than you, the reader, exist solely for the sake of your job or your career. After all, you, too, are a living entity. You exist to survive and thrive; working at your job is a means to that end. Similarly, returning investment to shareholders and serving customers are means to a similar end for IBM, Royal Dutch/Shell, Exxon, Procter & Gamble, General Motors, and every other company.

If the real purpose of a living company is to survive and thrive in the long run, then the priorities in managing such a company are very different from the values set forth in most of the modern academic business literature. Such a purpose also contradicts the views held by many managers and shareholders. To be sure, many management fashions resonate with the idea of a learning company—for example, the concepts of the "learning organization" and "knowledge as a strategic asset." But there are serious doubts that even the most enthusiastic managers and shareholders have fully explored the ramifications of these concepts.

The result: in today's increasingly volatile business environment, without the priorities of the living company, most managers will find that their companies do not have the habits to accomplish what they hope to achieve. On the other hand, exploring the ramifications of managing an entity that is alive, with the intent of handing it over to one's successors in better health than when one received it, is deeply gratifying. The owners of the firms in London's Tercentenarian Club and the managers of the Shell study survivors are usually exponents of a deeply felt corporate pride.

# LEARNING

# 1

# The Shift from Capitalism to a Knowledge Society

IF, AS A MANAGER, YOU TAKE THE FINDINGS OF THE ROYAL Dutch/Shell study or of Collins and Porras seriously, then you are faced with a seemingly insoluble dilemma. In the language of economics, companies are expected to operate with profits as their primary goal. On the other hand, as suggested by our studies, adopting this goal could well conflict with companies' longevity and life expectancy. Faced with this dilemma, managers often throw up their hands and choose the path of highest immediate return on investment, feeling that the survival of the company—and their jobs—will depend on following this path. Indeed, many managers at Shell and other companies have asked me why I would expect them to manage for the long run, with the risk of being dead in the short term.

My answer is: The dichotomy between profits and longevity is false. It is no longer necessary to choose between the two. *Corporate success and longevity are fundamentally interwoven, in a way that, nowadays, is qualitatively different from the relationship between success and longevity in the economic environment of five decades ago.* The twin policies of managing for profit and maximizing shareholder value, at the expense of all other goals, are vestigial management traditions. They no longer reflect the imperatives of the world we live in today. They are suboptimal, even destructive—not just to the rest of society, but to the companies that adopt them.

In short, the conventional management wisdom remains focused on the idea of conserving and maximizing capital. But during the past 50 years, the world of business has shifted from one dominated by capital to one dominated by knowledge. This shift explains the interest in organizational learning that has emerged in the last few years. Managers recognize that, unless their companies can accelerate the rate at which they learn, their primary asset will stagnate, and their competitors will outpace them.

Basic economic theory tells us that there have always been three key sources of wealth: land and natural resources, capital (the accumulation and reinvestment of possessions), and labor. The combination of those three creates the products and services that society needs for its material well-being. During most of human history, the critical factor of economic success was land. Those who could dominate and possess the land were guaranteed the controlling role in creating wealth. Thus owners of land, at least in Western society, were rich, and people who had no land were poor.

Then, as historians such as Fernand Braudel and Henri Pirenne have described in graphic detail, a dramatic shift took place between the late Middle Ages and the beginning of the twentieth century—a shift from land to capital as the primary factor in generating wealth.[1] The addition of more capital into the process of creating material wealth led to considerable increases in the effectiveness and efficiency of technological and commercial activity. Ships became bigger, voyages became longer, machines became more capable. By the end of the Middle Ages, much more money was available for such ends, at least in Western Europe. These savings were converted into the assets of the growing commercial ventures, which evolved into mining companies, shipping and trade enterprises, the first textile ateliers, and eventually modern corporations. The modern company, in short, developed when capital became available for the wealth-creating processes of the medieval tradesperson.

In the age of capital, wealth passed from those who controlled the land to those who controlled access to capital. The rich were no longer the landowners; they were the owners of capital. The ability to finance endeavors became the scarcest commodity of production.

Moreover, with the breakup of the old craft guilds and their evolution into companies, the owners of capital were able to control the
human production factor. In the language of economic theory, capital
was worth far more, and was far more scarce, than labor. Labor moved
from being part of the everyday life of human beings, an integral aspect
of the human community, to being a commodity, offered for sale on the
market. As Braudel put it in his book *The Wheels of Commerce:*

> All [a worker] had to offer was his arm or hand, his "labor"
> in other words. And of course his intelligence or skill. The phe-
> nomenon can be seen with unusual clarity in the case of the
> miners of Central Europe. Having long been independent
> artisans, working in small groups, they were obliged in the
> fifteenth and sixteenth century to put themselves under the
> control of the merchants who alone could provide the consid-
> erable investment required for equipment to mine deep below
> the surface. And they became wage-earners.[2]

Over the course of the following centuries, a new element emerged
in management thinking. If a company fell into trouble, jobs were cut
first, because the capital assets (and the investors' goodwill) were far
more scarce and valuable, and managers saw the optimization of capital as their first priority. During the Great Depression of the 1930s, for
example, it had been considered good banking practice to liquidate and
destroy client institutions, and all the jobs associated with them, if this
would help recover even a scrap of invested capital. (This may have
seemed harsh, but it was necessary. Capital-supplying institutions were
a lot less robust than they are nowadays, and they were fighting for
their own survival.[3]) In their attitude toward capital, companies were
far different from their older siblings, the church and the military. Even
in the grim retreat at Dunkirk during the second world war, the British
expeditionary force scuttled their war machines to save their soldiers.
Capital assets were not as important as people.

Sometime over the course of the twentieth century, the Western nations moved out of the age of capital, however, and into the age of
knowledge. Few managers recognized it at the time, but *capital was losing its scarcity.* After the second world war, an enormous capital accumulation began. Individuals and banks and companies became much

more resilient. Technology also began to change, thanks to telecommunications, television, computers, and commercial air travel, with the effect of making capital far more fungible and resilient, easier to move around—and consequently less scarce.

With capital easily available, the critical production factor shifted to people. But it did not shift to simple labor. *Instead, knowledge displaced capital as the scarce production factor—the key to corporate success.* Those who had knowledge and knew how to apply it would henceforth be the wealthiest members of society: the technological specialists, investment bankers, creative artists, and facilitators of new understanding. This was not merely a function of the need for people to supply technical skills, under the direction of their bosses. The growing complexity of work created a need for people to be a source of inventiveness, and to become distributors and evaluators of inventions and knowledge, through the whole work community. Judgment, on behalf of the company as a whole, could no longer be the exclusive prerogative of a few people at the top.[4]

Had we known where to look, even back in the 1950s we could have seen the shift of value from capital to knowledge. It was becoming visible in the rise of asset-poor, brain-rich companies and partnerships—international auditor firms, management consultancies, and advertising and media businesses. Within a decade or two, even these would be eclipsed by the explosively growing software and information technology companies. All of these brain-rich companies cannot be managed in the old asset-oriented style. Their managers have had to shift their priorities, from running companies to optimize capital, to running companies to optimize people. People, in these companies, are the carriers of knowledge and therefore the source of competitive advantage.

## Economic Success versus Learning

In the early 1950s, during the beginning of the shift from capital to knowledge, I was a business school student at Erasmus University in Rotterdam. I can distinctly remember the definition of business that they taught us there. This "economic company," as I now call it, was a very comforting entity. It was rational, calculable, and controllable:

> Companies produce goods and services, for which other people are prepared to pay a price, by trying to find the optimum combination of the three production factors—labor, capital and land. These three are substitutable. Labor can be replaced by capital, for example. The optimum combination of the production factors is the one at which the company is producing the goods and services at minimum costs to be sold at maximum price for the maximization of profits.[5]

This definition has great clarity. Many people will recognize it as the way they have been told to think about companies. The definition is also clear in distinguishing between successful and unsuccessful companies. Success equals maximum profits at the optimum combination of the production factors. The definition makes it not only easy to measure success, but quick. You do not have to wait 50 years to find out whether you have been successful. At the end of each quarter of each year, you can measure success from the quarterly results. And your company might win the corporate equivalent of an Oscar when *Fortune* magazine and the *Financial Times* publish their lists of the 100 or 500 Chosen Ones. To have the highest return on capital employed, the highest turnover, the highest market capitalization—those are the criteria of success under the economic definition.

We students of the 1950s, fledgling examples of *Homo economicus,* learned this definition enthusiastically. We did not realize that, already, it was an inaccurate description of true corporate success. I now realize that I had my first inkling of this inaccuracy after leaving Erasmus, when I entered my first place of work: the Shell refinery near Rotterdam. Soon, after I walked in the door, I felt a slight level of discomfort. The theories back at business school had mentioned labor, but there had been no talk of people. Yet the real world, the refinery, seemed to be full of them. And because the workplace was full of people, it looked suspiciously as if companies were not always rational, calculable, and controllable.

Today, I recognize that the economic company is an abstraction with little to do with the reality of corporate life. Not only does labor not equate with people, but the emphasis on profits and on the maximization of shareholder value ignores the two most significant forces acting on companies today: the shift to knowledge as the critical production factor and the changing world around the companies.

Companies could act according to the economic definition of success when managers felt that they were in control of their world. But rare is the manager who feels in control of today's turbulent environment. Therefore, to cope with a changing world, any entity must develop the capability of shifting and changing, of developing new skills and attitudes: in short, the capability of learning. As we will see in this book, the essence of learning is the ability to manage change by changing yourself—as much for people when they grow up as for companies when they live through turmoil. The pioneering learning theorist Jean Piaget called this form of change "learning through accommodation."[6] Its essence, he said, was to change one's internal structure to remain in harmony with a changed environment.

This gives us an entirely different imperative for corporate success. A successful company is one that can *learn* effectively.

## When Success Is Based on Learning

Under this definition, people are much more critical to a company. Knowledge, after all, is carried in the heads of people. This is not to say that capital assets are unimportant. They are vital. Without capital, mankind would have never reached the economic output we have got. But the current way of thinking about companies frames the issue as an either-or question: If you are promoting the interests of people, then you are necessarily shortchanging the interests of capital. From a learning orientation, the nurturing of people and the nurturing of capital reinforce each other.

During the 1980s, I saw a debate occur with great regularity inside the Shell Group. How could we best improve our return on investment? The usual response, at senior executive levels, was "Overheads must come down." In Shell, as in all large corporations, 80 percent of the overhead costs relate to the expenses of people. The outcome of these discussions was therefore inevitable. A number of people would have to be let go. The rest of our managerial attention then went into figuring out how this reduction would be achieved. Which functions or regions would be cut? Would we cut through staff transfers, voluntary redundancy, or enforced dismissal?

During one such debate, I remember the lone voice of Ian McCutcheon, the group controller, asking, "But what about the loss of human potential, experience, and loyalty?" I also remember how this remark disappeared in the wind. No serious attempt was made to consider the potential for increasing future proceeds; everyone focused attention on the immediate prospect of reducing costs.

The same debate takes place in many companies today, and in many of these companies, the concerns about human capital are lost in much the same manner. That is why we need a new way of thinking about the measurement of success in our companies. By outsiders, we are judged and measured in economic terms: return on investment and capital assets. But within the company, our success depends on our skill with human beings: building and developing the consistent knowledge base of our enterprise.

Personally, I'm inclined to believe that the sharp difference between these two definitions—the economic company definition and the learning company definition—lies at the core of the crisis managers face today. The tension between them is almost certainly one of the key reasons behind the surprisingly low average life expectancy of companies in the northern hemisphere.

On one hand, all the experts, academics, and managerial success measurements line up on the side of the economic definition. They suggest that the company's heart, the core of its nature, is the economic activity it pursues to stay alive. On the other hand is the evidence of managers' own eyes, ears, and feelings: that the core of their company's nature, its heart, is its existence as a continuous work community—in short, as a living, learning company.

To make the case for a noneconomic company credible, then, we need to look more closely at learning in organizations. What links can we draw between the idea of a living company, acting in its own self-interest as an entity unto itself, and the idea of a learning company, with sensitivity to its environment?

# 2

# The Memory of the Future

LEARNING BEGINS WITH PERCEPTION. NEITHER AN INDIVIDUAL nor a company will even begin to learn without having seen something of interest in the environment. That is why surviving and thriving in a volatile world requires, first of all, management that is sensitive to its company's environment. At least a few of the company's leaders should be attentive and responsive to the world in which they live, even to the extent of playing an active role in that outside world. Navel gazers are necessary in every company, but they see little of the forces that will affect the future of that company.

By contrast, an open and extroverted management will perceive whatever is happening outside much earlier. Only after seeing that something is about to change (or has already begun to change) outside the company will management be ready to deal with the effects of that change. Many of these effects lie in the future and are uncertain. In the desire to "know" and reduce that uncertainty, most managers spend far too much time on the relatively useless question: What will happen to us?

But managers who perceive change early should spend more time on a far more useful question: What will we *do* if such-and-such happens? Only this latter question can lead managers to make changes inside the company that will allow it to survive and thrive in the new world. Indeed, as experience shows, fundamental and painful change may be necessary, possibly even including the abolition of a company's core business.

In fact, at Royal Dutch/Shell in 1983, our study of long-lived large companies provided many examples of the fundamental nature of the internal changes needed for companies to survive in a turbulent environment. The study was initially triggered by the ever-present disquiet in any natural resource company: What will happen when the oil runs out? To our relief, we found that no company we studied, in all of our literature research, had ever failed because its key natural resource was depleted. Yet many companies had switched away from their original natural resource base or their original business. DuPont is a classic, well-known example. Its business portfolio had moved, over time, from gunpowder to chemicals via the majority shareholding in General Motors.

After the Shell study team reported this sort of finding, I found myself asking it another question: Had any of our large, longstanding companies changed in fundamental ways—not because they were forced to, but because they anticipated the need for changes?

Indeed they had. *Most* of the long-lived companies, according to the team, had anticipated the need for change at least once during their lives. More often than not, this opportunity was born of a crisis, amid a new threat from the business environment—a new competitor, a trade restriction, a shift in the marketplace, or a rival technology. The long-lived companies seemed to have an innate ability to exploit these crises and turn them into new business. Frequently, someone within the enterprise would identify the crisis ahead of time, but not as a crisis; it was a new opportunity, an alternative avenue for company growth and profitability. Here again, DuPont was an example. Its leaders, mostly family members, had astutely navigated the technological, political, and social cross-currents of nineteenth- and twentieth-century America. The company took an early lead with dynamite production in America, and later with cellophane packaging and plastics research. Some members of the du Pont family, the family that owned and managed the company, had become prominent politicians—including U.S.

Congressman and Governor Pierre S. du Pont IV. Ethel du Pont had married Theodore Roosevelt, Jr. And there was evidence that this sensitivity had permitted the family decision makers to move rapidly from one business to another, consolidating their position in General Motors and the chemical industries in time for the industrial expansion of World War II.[1]

As we put it in our report:

> Identifying the opportunity or the threat was one matter; stimulating the change necessary to take advantage of the opportunity was another. There is a considerable difference between companies that stared blindly at threat and opportunity and those that reacted and changed.[2]

What gave the companies the ability to accomplish this? We will return to that question throughout this book, for it depended on all four distinctions of a living company: its adaptiveness to the outside world (learning), its character and identity (persona), its relationships with people and institutions inside and around itself (ecology), and the way it developed over time (evolution). We could see that the most accessible of these capabilities, and the one which often came first, was learning. The long-lived companies were *sensitive* to their community and their environment. This sensitivity was not soft or driven by social responsibility. It was driven by the living company's self-interest.

> Behind all displays of sensitivity to the community [we wrote in our report] there generally lay a hard headed approach and a recognition that . . . alertness and responsiveness . . . helped create the climate in which business growth could take place.[3]

Consider, for example, the case of the Swedish company Stora. If you feel overwhelmed by the turbulence in your business environment today, then think of the shifting forces with which Stora had to cope. The first written mention of the company dates from 1288. In those days it was a copper mine based in Dalecarlia, a province of central Sweden.

When it was a mere 270 years old, during the fifteenth century, the company had to fight the king of Sweden to maintain its independence and identity. Kings throughout Europe, enmeshed in the struggle to establish centralized nation-states, were grasping for every penny they could lay their hands on, and their demands threatened the existence of enterprises like Stora. Thus Stora took on a political role within Sweden, drawing not just on its leaders' financial resources, but also on significant support from peasant workers in its home base, the province of Dalecarlia. Ultimately, the master miners of Stora found an appropriate answer to external turbulence in the manner with which they organized themselves. As one historian wrote, "A Guild was established at the Mountain . . . adopting an independent and militaristic profile. For the members, loyalty to the Guild superseded the law of the land, and the word of the Master of the Guild weighed heavier than that of a judge."[4]

During that period of unrest, it would have been catastrophic for the company to concentrate on its business in an introverted fashion, oblivious to politics. Instead, the company reshaped its goals and methods to match the demands of the world outside. It did the same thing again and again, throughout the centuries, from the Middle Ages through the Reformation, into the wars of the 1600s, the Industrial Revolution, and two world wars in the twentieth century. To appreciate the difficulties of adaptation, consider how little data were available to the Swedish managers of Stora. Instead of telephones, airplanes, and electronic networks, they had to depend on runners, horsemen, and ships to carry messages. They barely had the facilities for a global view of their business, let alone a view of the global business environment. Nor, apparently, did their boards have the time to spend deliberating the needs and demands of society. Yet timely reaction to the conditions in society was necessary for the survival of the company and sometimes even of its individual members.

Over the next several centuries, while it coped with shifting social and political forces, the company continually shifted its business, moving from copper to forest exploitation, to iron smelting to hydro power and eventually to paper, wood pulp, and chemicals. Its production technologies also shifted—from steam to internal combustion, then to electricity, and ultimately to the microchip.

Each one of these changes, in hindsight, seems herculean, but for the people running these enterprises in those days they may well have been gradual and almost imperceptible at the outset. Certainly, some of these changes must have involved a crisis at the root of the company, but Stora—and every other successful company we studied—managed to effect its dramatic changes *without sacrificing its corporate identity or corporate life in the process.* This can mean only one thing: these companies reacted early rather than later, by foresight rather than by catch-up.

## Changing to Match the Outside World

Today, businesspeople ignore public attitudes on such issues as national sovereignty, colonialism and imperialism, pollution, conservation, exploitation, "the decline of the middle class," and even free trade at their peril. Social changes—such as the changing position of women in society, the growth in leisure, shifts in transport, and the evolution of consumer taste—continually create new employment opportunities and new markets, while old markets falter. Economic indicators rise and fall wildly, including international currency rates, inflation rates, interest rates, and product life cycles (led by the electronics industry). Shareholder attitudes change from docile to demanding and sometimes back again. With the fall of the Berlin Wall, we have seen political changes that undo the hegemony of 70 years of communism in some countries. All of these attitudes are key aspects of a company's business environment.

When I say "environment," I do not use the word as an ecologist might, to refer to natural surroundings. Rather, I use it to mean the sum total of all forces that affect a company's actions. In the last 20 years, that business environment, within which all companies must operate, has shown oscillations of increasing frequency and amplitude. These, in turn, reorient the corporate sense of purpose. In the heat of restructuring and reengineering, it's often easy to lose sight of the *purpose* of the change: to meet the changing pressures from the outside world.

There are times when a company's know-how, product range, and labor relations are in harmony with the world around it. The situations are familiar; the company is well organized, trained, and prepared. The managers do not need to develop and implement new concepts. During those times, the essence of management is to allocate resources to promote growth and development. This is a very gratifying type of work. It means channeling capital and human talent to those parts of the organization that are best placed to benefit from the converging harmonious environment—and these parts of the organization return the compliment by becoming larger, better established, and more powerful within the firm.

But then comes the inevitable moment, just when the company has neatly organized itself to cope with the previous situation, when the current business environment diverges. It becomes disharmonious with the way management had structured the company—particularly with the large, well-established, powerful components that benefited from the previous structure. If this disharmony is of a fundamental enough nature, then fundamental changes are required in the company as well.

*Continuous, fundamental changes in the external world—a turbulent business environment—require continuous management for change in the company. This means making continuous fundamental changes in the internal structures of the company.* For many psychologists, this principle represents one important aspect of learning.

This imperative also has important consequences for the way we run our companies. The company must be able, when necessary, to alter its marketing, its product range, where and how it does its manufacturing, and its organizational form—to stay in harmony with the surrounding world. A fundamental revision in finance regulations can lead a bank to consider new markets and new products, dramatically stretching its existing capabilities. An increase in oil prices (which an oil marketing company might treat as routine) can force an airline into a fundamental revision of its costs, its price structure, its flight schedules, or the composition of its fleet (to more fuel-efficient aircraft). Once these new solutions have been implemented, whether they involve a new technology, marketing policy, project portfolio, or service schedule, the company is no longer the same. It has moved into a new phase of its life. This is the essence of learning.

To accomplish this type of learning, the company must see clearly what is happening in its environment. Once again, learning begins with perception. How else can managers know when significant change is necessary, or how to act effectively to achieve a new sort of harmony? Yet corporate managers, enmeshed in the details of their change efforts, often think about their outside pressures in only the vaguest terms. They do not *see;* they do not develop a careful sensitivity to the signals of pressures outside the firm and how those pressures are changing.

Why is it so difficult for managers to maintain their sensitivity? Why do companies fail to see the signals of change ahead of time? In my last assignment in the Shell Group, as coordinator of corporate planning, it was important to find an answer to that question. If companies could see early and manage internal change by foresight, a great deal of capital destruction and social misery would be prevented—not only in our company, but in any company. Why, then, are so many companies seemingly so blind and deaf to what is happening around them?

Over time, five different answers to that question emerged. The first two or three of them have probably occurred to you; they represent the unspoken, but prevalent, myths about why managers fail to perceive effectively.

## Theory 1:
## Managers Are Stupid

Business commentators and academics, with the benefit of hindsight, imply or suggest that managers are idiots—either blind, deaf, or plain stupid. Otherwise, why did the great American railway companies not see the highways for motorcars being built alongside their tracks in the beginning of this century? Why did the makers of Western consumer electronics fail to foresee the Japanese and Korean competitors who would engulf them? Clearly, businesspeople are not intellectually equipped to cope with the changing nature of their environment.

I have never liked this explanation. The great majority of people I meet in business circles are neither deaf, blind, nor stupid. In any case, the problem managers face is not acting intelligently in isolation, but tapping all of the company's intelligence to foresee problems together.

## Theory 2:
## We Can See Only When a Crisis Opens Our Eyes

I put the question to a number of psychologists: Why do managers fail to exercise foresight? They explained that there is a human resistance to change—a resistance which is basically good, for both the individual and society. One should not change for change's sake. However, said these psychologists, in effect, when change is demanded for survival, this resistance must be overcome and the only way for this to happen is through pain—deep, prolonged pain!

The corporate equivalent of pain is a crisis. In the heat of a lengthy crisis, according to this theory, people in the organization will feel the pain and be convinced that something must be done. Indeed, you will often hear managers say, "What this company needs is a nice little crisis. Then we'll be able to get some change around here."

There is no denying that many a fundamental change had a crisis at its roots. Whenever I talk to managers of a company that went through structural adaptation, they always remember clearly how painful a time they had in the period preceding the changes. And this is true not only for companies. Think of OPEC in 1986, many trade unions during the last decade, and the former Soviet Union as it struggles through its current transition. In each case, the world around them changed. Warnings were ignored until, finally, the disharmony began to show up (in companies) in the quarterly results (when it is almost too late anyway). Even then, the old objectives were doggedly pursued. Belts were tightened. Jobs were lost. People struggled under the stress. Ultimately, the institution's survival was at stake. And finally, grudgingly, people began to adopt an orientation of learning.

Despite the stress involved, many managers enjoy a crisis. At last, it is possible to *do* things. Because time is of the essence, at last the company can move without consultations and lengthy deliberations. Autocratic, heroic management thrives. Decisions must be made quickly. Power is centralized and concentrated—pulled inward and upward into a few heads: the company "goes for broke."

But does that mean that crises are the *only* avenue for learning? Or that crises *necessarily* produce learning? One can think of a great many crises in which little institutional adaptation took place at all: companies wilt under the pressure of a hostile takeover, a fierce new competitor, or an unexpected lawsuit. These crises tend to follow the same generic pattern.

* At some point, as prospects worsen, the damage or danger becomes evident, and a consensus, grudgingly or not, develops about the inevitability of change.
* When that happens, there is little time left.
* Because there is little time, few options remain open. They are not necessarily the best options; they are limited to those that require little *time* to implement.
* Almost by definition, these tend to be the tough options, devastating to morale and difficult to pull off with corporate identity intact: improve cash flow drastically, cut costs, cut capital expenditures, cut staff.
* The crisis is a self-reinforcing cycle. The more deeply you become enmeshed, the more options you must forgo, and the more you run out of time—which cuts your possibilities further and enmeshes you more deeply in the crisis. To act by foresight would surely be superior.

But can fundamental change be brought about by foresight? In practice, this can happen only if the company's managers can see the signals for change in time—before the situation has deteriorated to the point where the company is losing options. *In short, to act with foresight, the company must act on signals, rather than on pain.*

In the end, the psychologist's view—that the only way to obtain a fundamental change is by way of a crisis—is a pessimistic one which I have difficulty accepting. It means that, faced with a disharmonious environment, there is nothing that a manager can do on his or her own. Events follow their inescapable road to disaster. Business life is a gamble or, rather, a Greek tragedy. We suffer and cope. There is no hope for improvement.

## Theory 3:
## We Can See Only What We Have Already Experienced

With the emergence of cognitive psychology and the study of mental maps, some psychologists began to claim that people can only "see" what they have experienced before—at least in some respect. To receive a signal from the outside world, it must match some matrix already in the mind, placed there by previous events.

Consider, for example, the story of the tribal chief who was brought to Singapore by a group of British explorers at the beginning of this century. The explorers had found him deep in the high mountains of the Malaysian peninsula, in an isolated valley. His tribe was literally still in the Stone Age. Its people had not even invented the wheel. Nonetheless, the chief was highly intelligent, and a delightful man to talk to (once they made themselves understood). He seemed to have a deep, meaningful perception of his own world.

So, as an experiment, they decided to convey him to Singapore. It was at the time already a sophisticated seaport, with multistory buildings and a harbor with big ships. Economically, it had a market economy with traders and professional specializations. Socially, it had many more layers than the society from which the tribal chief came. They marched the chief through this world for 24 hours, submitting him to thousands of signals of potential change for his own society. Then they brought him back to his mountain valley and started to debrief him.

Of all the wonders he had seen, only one seemed important to him: He had seen a man carrying more bananas than he had ever thought one man could carry. What the mind has not experienced before, it cannot see. The tribal chief could not relate to multistory buildings or giant ships; but when he saw a market vendor pushing a cart laden with bananas, he could make sense of it. All the other signs of potential change were so far outside his previous life experiences that his mind could not grasp what his eyes were telling him.

There is some truth to this explanation. But it cannot be the only explanation for why companies fail to see signals of change in their environment. It would mean that old companies with rich histories would always prevail over young ones, at least when it came to being flexible, because the old companies would have built up a much greater store of experience from which to draw meaningful links with new perceptions.

Actually, I believe this dynamic does take place. An older company with a good institutional memory will probably see more than a young company. Nevertheless, old and experienced companies consistently miss the signals. As the statistics convincingly show, they are just as prone to crisis as newer companies.

Some other factor must be at work.

## Theory 4:
## We Cannot See What Is Emotionally Difficult to See

In the oil industry, we saw the value of sensitivity first hand during three major crises of the 1970s and 1980s: the OPEC oil supply crisis of 1973, the overthrow of the shah of Iran in 1979, and the collapse of the oil price in 1986. In every large company, at least a few people anticipated these crises and warned about them in advance. Nonetheless, most of the companies failed to implement the required internal changes in time. By the mid-1980s, this lack of foresight had taken its toll, with the result that two of the "Seven Sisters"—the major oil companies that had seemed impregnable and unstoppable in the early 1970s—had been weakened or had merged. Many smaller oil companies also died.

What happened to them? One key factor was the rise and fall of exploration and production (E&P)—the high-tech component of oil companies which drills for oil, pumps it from the ground, and sells it as crude oil. In the 1973 supply crisis (known in America as the OPEC oil embargo), the price of crude oil soared to hitherto unknown heights. It remained high for 13 more years. Although this represented a real crisis for just about everybody, both inside and outside the oil companies, it was not a crisis at all for E&P. Their product had suddenly gone up in price from $2 per barrel to $30 per barrel—a very harmonious synchronization with the outside world for them.

This harmonious situation resulted in a distinct shift in resource allocation. Once, perhaps 30 percent of an oil company's overall budget might have gone to E&P. Now this department would receive 50 percent, or, in some companies, 70 percent. Careers of existing E&P managers were buoyed by success, and new, capable people went into E&P because that was where the success was. As a result, at major oil companies, top executives increasingly came out of E&P backgrounds.

Then came 1986. Suddenly the oil price fell back to about $10 per barrel. For E&P in particular, this was a very disharmonious crash. Worse still, the oil companies had now reorganized themselves around the leadership of E&P. They had successfully responded to harmony, but they found disharmony much more difficult. The thinking of top leaders was colored by their E&P background, and E&P continued to take the lion's share of resources. They could not provide the same level of return on those resources, but neither could they change their methods and approaches. At many companies, they reinforced their resistance to change with wishful thinking: "Things will turn around and the oil price will become 'normal' again."

To make fundamental change was emotionally difficult. For one thing, E&P managers at many oil companies had to come to terms with the fact that their priorities and knowledge were no longer the determining sources of triumph. Moreover, the companies discovered that managing for fundamental internal change is inherently far less gratifying than managing for growth. In a nongrowth environment, you no longer manage by allocating an ever-expanding pool of resources. Now you have to cut costs; you learn about frugality; and you seek new business with much greater risks, much less room for error, and much more uncertain rewards.

Understandably enough, those who have become used to the high emotions of the previous phase will resist correction in this phase. Switching direction is never fun for the people who were at the front of the previous charge. Consequently, the newspapers are full of examples of companies that, under conditions of diverging environment, postpone changing their (previously successful) policies for far too long—until they slide into a deepening crisis.

You cannot do anything to remove this emotional pain. It is a necessary complement of fundamental change. And, indeed, it is powerful. But it cannot be overwhelming, for otherwise companies would never change. And, as we can see from the example of Stora, some do. There is, contrary to the pessimistic views of these theories, enormous hope for improvement.

In addition, human beings seem to have developed a much better capability for foresight than companies. Thus, after considering the first four theories during my inquiry at Shell, we began to look into the cognitive nature of human adaptability. What did psychological researchers believe was the factor that gave human beings their ability to anticipate the future? And could companies emulate this aspect of human behavior?

## Theory 5:
## We Can See Only What Is Relevant to Our View of the Future

At Shell, this inquiry eventually led us to the work of David Ingvar, the head of the neurobiology department at the University of Lund (Sweden).[5] The results of his research, published in 1985, show that the human brain is constantly attempting to make sense of the future. Every moment of our lives, we instinctively create action plans and programs for the future—anticipating the moment at hand, the next minutes, the emerging hours, the following days, the ongoing weeks, and the anticipated years to come—in one part of our mind. This brain activity takes place throughout the daytime, independent of what else we are doing; it occurs in even more concentrated form at night, during sleep.

You have probably created a dozen or more such time paths during the time you have been reading this chapter. "If I continue reading for another hour, it will be too late to telephone Margaret. Then I'll have to leave to see Andrew before dinner. If Andrew offers me a drink, I might be too late to call Marcia before she goes to the theater. It would be better to call her tomorrow morning anyway. On the other hand, if I stop reading now, I could still go to town by train. If the train arrives late, I'll phone from the station and then take a cab, rather than the subway. . . ."

These plans are sequentially organized, as series of potential actions: "If this happens, I will do that." These are not *predictions*. They do not pretend to tell what *will* happen. They are time paths into an anticipated future. Each combines a future hypothetical condition of the environment ("if the train arrives late") with an option for action ("I'll take a cab").

Not only does the brain make those time paths in the prefrontal lobes, it stores them. We visit these futures and remember our visits. We have, in other words, a "memory of the future," continually being formed and optimized in our imaginations and revisited time and time again. The memory of the future, as Ingvar calls it, is an internal process within the brain, related to man's language ability and to perception. It apparently helps us sort through the plethora of images and sensations coming into the brain, by assigning relevance to them. We perceive something as meaningful if it fits meaningfully with a memory that we have made of an anticipated future.

Ingvar remarks that among "normal" people, about 60 percent of these anticipated futures are favorable: good things happen in them. And 40 percent are dire. If the balance is disturbed, you get perennial optimists or incorrigible pessimists, depending on whether their prevailing memories of the future are positive or negative. In any case, the healthier the brain, the more alternative time paths it makes, striking a reasonable balance between favorable conditions and unfavorable ones. We make and store a great many options for the future, far more than we will ever fulfill.

In his research, David Ingvar addresses the question of what function this sort of "memory of the future" might serve. Why would it have evolved? An obvious reason would be to prepare us for action once one of the visited futures materializes. But Ingvar suggests another purpose: as a filter, to help deal with the information overload to which every human being is constantly subjected.

The human body, notes Ingvar, has a plethora of sensory channels: the eyes, ears, nose, taste buds, and every part of the skin. Each one of those sensors sends a continuous stream of signals about the surrounding world to the brain. So much random information reaches the brain that the vast majority of it must be ignored. The brain could not function properly if it gave equal priority to all the information it receives. Ingvar hypothesizes that our "memories of the future" provide a subconscious guide to help us determine which incoming information is relevant. The stored time paths serve as templates against which the incoming signals are measured. If the incoming information fits one of the alternative time paths, the input is understood. Information becomes knowledge, and the signal acquires meaning.

The message from this research is clear. We will not perceive a signal from the outside world unless it is relevant to an option for the future that we have already worked out in our imaginations. The more "memories of the future" we develop, the more open and receptive we will be to signals from the outside world.

If learning begins with perception, then Ingvar's theory has important implications for management that is trying to guide its company through a turbulent environment. Ingvar is, in fact, saying that the act of perception is not simply a matter of collecting information—of looking at an object and noting all sorts of observations and data about it. Perception, to a human being, is an active engagement with the world. And, in a company, it is similarly active. Perception requires the deliberate effort by management groups within the company to "visit their future" and develop time paths and options. Otherwise, the observations and data that one has collected will have no meaning.

Making this effort is easier for an individual human being than for a company, because the brain is hard-wired to perform this sort of active engagement. Imagine that a man living in France has taken his car to London by ferry on a business visit. At eight o'clock the next morning, he drives his car from the hotel to the office. While subjected to the considerable information overload that stems from trying to find his way through rush hour traffic in a strange town, he switches on the radio to hear the news. Even more signals reach the brain. At the end of the newscast, the announcer briefly mentions that a strike has been announced for the ferry port of Dover.

Most of us would not even hear this piece of information. But our French resident has a time path stored in his mind. He has a memory of the future, seeing himself taking his car that very night to Dover to catch a ferry. He hears the signal, because it is relevant to that memory. Information has become knowledge.

A company is not hard-wired to produce this sort of memory of the future. Management must take specific action to produce one. That is why David Ingvar's theory is so significant in pointing toward a means of improving a company's powers of perception. His theory explains, to my satisfaction at least, why managers do not recognize external events in time to avoid crisis. And Ingvar's theory also suggests that corporations can develop the sensitivity they need, by finding ways to build up an organizational "memory of the future."

# 3

# Tools for Foresight

FEW COMPANIES ARE AS CAPABLE AS HUMAN BEINGS AT DEALING with the future. Managers may see signals of a potential future and even talk about it together. But the managers and the companies still do not respond in timely fashion to that future, even after it has occurred.

Could it be that this difficulty exists because companies are trying to deal with the future by predicting it? Predicting the future is very different from creating the sorts of alternative time paths into the future that David Ingvar's work suggests. Back in Chapter 1, "The Shift from Capitalism to a Knowledge Society," we noted that some management teams ask, "What will happen to us?" They are engaged in prediction. Other management teams ask, "What will we do, if such-and-such happens?" They are engaged in alternative time paths, particularly when that question is put on the agenda of a meeting of a corporate board with decision-making power.

By reverting to predictions as a standard way of thinking about the future, the corporate powers of perception remain greatly reduced. That leads them to the same conundrum faced by the mayor of Rotterdam, in a parable which we found very meaningful in Group Planning at Royal Dutch/Shell.[1]

Imagine that it is 1920, and you have somehow been granted absolute power to predict the future. You happen to visit the mayor of Rotterdam, and during that time, you describe in vivid detail what is going to happen to his town during the next 25 years. Thus, during an otherwise perfectly normal working day, the mayor hears about the advent of the Weimar Republic, hyperinflation, the 1929 stock exchange crash, the Great Depression that followed, the rise of Nazism in Germany with its (for Rotterdam) damaging economic policies of autarchy, the outbreak of the second world war, the carpet-bombing of the town's city center, and, finally, the systematic destruction of the town's port installations during the calamitous winter of 1945.

The mayor listens to this information placidly. He gives every sign of believing you. And then he asks, "If you were in my shoes, hearing all this, amid all the other opinions and facts that reach me during the course of my day, what do you reasonably expect me to *do* about this information?"

What is reasonable to expect the mayor to do?

When I ask this question in discussion groups, we always reach the same answer: There is *nothing* the mayor can be expected to do. Even if he gives your prediction a higher degree of credibility than most of the other information that reached him, he would have neither the courage nor the powers of persuasion to take the far-reaching decisions required by such a prediction.

*The future cannot be predicted. But, even if it could, we would not dare to act on the prediction.*

Most people accept this thesis in a cool, academic debate. Nevertheless, in real life there is an insatiable demand for predictions. The yearning for some certainty about the future is so strong that most of us will at times act against our better judgment and demand some precise prediction of the future. That is why there are worldwide industries that supply information about the future—from fortune-tellers and astrologers to consultants, academics, and economists. These are industries rich in euphemisms, in which the product is often wrapped in sheets of fine print and jargon which the customer does not normally read. But that doesn't matter anyway, because few people with real responsibilities dare take decisions based on the information, even though they eagerly asked (and paid) for it in the first place.

Perhaps we can understand the corporate demand for prediction better by looking at the *individual* demand. There is a huge market, for example, for astrological forecasts—in which some highly successful suppliers try to satisfy an almost-insatiable demand for the feeling of reduced uncertainty. One of those highly successful suppliers has been the British astrologer Patrick Walker, syndicated worldwide through Rupert Murdoch's news corporation. The Murdoch syndicate in New York estimates Walker's audience to consist of at least a billion people.[2]

From the perspective of decision making, interviews with Walker himself are fascinating. He describes his brand of popular newspaper astrology as a sort of weather forecast and finds it hard to explain why people believe that he is such a good astrologer. "Perhaps it is because I try not to make rigid predictions. . . . [A]strology has got nothing to do with your marriage breaking up. You are the one that breaks up the marriage. . . . All I can do is highlight the circumstances. How you behave is up to you."

One would think that an astrologer's methods deserve little attention when contemplating the serious subject of interpreting the future for business decisions. Yet it is interesting to contrast Walker's view with the approach implicitly taken by many financial forecasting systems. Patrick Walker leaves room for free will; he tells his audience that they, at least in part, will shape their own future. Corporate and government planners, by contrast, imply (or pretend) that the future is a fatalistic *given*. No action by management will make any difference in the way the future will unfold. The job of the planner is to divine the "right" future as closely as possible. And the managers, when faced with their own bad decisions, use the excuse that they were given the wrong prediction!

This is abdication of managerial responsibility: dealing with the future can never be delegated. It is the uncomfortable component of the manager's job. It is one of the reasons why senior executives are paid their high salaries.

Daniel Yergin, author of the Pulitzer prizewinning history of oil *The Prize*,[3] found exactly this sort of resistance in the oil industry during the mid-1980s. In 1985, he once told me, there was much apprehension in oil company boardrooms that the price of crude oil could crash dramatically. But he did not know of any company in which the senior leaders had addressed the question: What will we *do* if the price should fall?

It is always easy for managers to try to predict. It is always tempting to address at great length the question: What will happen to us? Will the oil price fall? Will our competitors expand into our business? Will the Soviet empire disband or the South African government change? Will the technology we use become obsolete? Like a great many advisers to an imaginary mayor of Rotterdam, managers tend to spend many hours comfortably debating the likelihood of one future or another, without arriving at any conclusion.

Imagine, instead, if managers asked themselves, "What would we do if such-and-such happened? Suppose the oil price fell (or rose)? How would we react? Suppose our competitors expanded? Suppose there were a change in government or a shift in our technologies? What would be our response? Answering these questions, or questions like them, would allow managers to work out one or more of David Ingvar's mental time paths. It would allow us to build ourselves a series of memories of the future—anticipations of events that might or might not take place.

Thereafter, we would be prepared. We would have thought about our course and played it out in our imaginations. We would not have to try to predict the future, because we could rely on our memory of the many futures that we have already visited.

## Planning and the Illusion of Certainty

Back in the 1930s, the corporate world made its first serious attempt to deal systematically with the future. A series of "tools for foresight" were developed, under the generic name of "planning." Over the next three decades, every line manager learned to incorporate the output from these planning tools into his or her decision making. Yet, as we have just seen, "planning" does not usually mean learning to anticipate possible futures, build "memories" of them, and prepare ourselves for them. Instead, planning is typically seen as the work of reducing uncertainty through prediction.

When I was first exposed to planning, as a student shortly after World War II, the task of reducing uncertainty was organized so that trained specialists would handle it. By about 1940, many companies had begun to hand over the task of worrying about the future to the "back-room boys" in the planning department. The more pragmatic characters on the line could thus "get on with the job," without having to waste valuable time imagining possible events. Management was thus split between "those who do" and "those who plan."

In most companies, this specialized planning activity found a home in the finance function or, more precisely, in accounting. In retrospect, this was the worst possible environment for developing "memories of the future," but by the standards of corporate practice, it was a perfectly logical place for the new profession of planners to land. Financial-based planning promises to provide a great deal of factual, quantified information about the future, in a form (figures and money) that is highly beguiling and suggestive of precision.

When given something new to do, most people begin by doing what they already know how to do well. Thus, when asked to satisfy the company's yearning for knowledge about the future, the accountants of corporate finance began with their strengths: their ability to make balance sheets and profit-and-loss accounts. They set out to predict next year's budgets, balance sheets, and P&L accounts based on estimates of next year's sales and operating costs. They calculated whether the company would be short of money or have some surplus one year into the future. Elegantly collated in a binder, the final estimate provided the company's "doers" with a quantified report—useless, but compelling—on how tomorrow, next month, or next year would look.

There was one useful aspect to this exercise, however. In the process of compiling their information, the accountants had to think quite hard about what was happening in the outside world. People who have to estimate next year's sales will find themselves thinking: What will the economic activity be? Will the GNP grow, or will there be a recession? To answer such questions seriously, one must come up with some idea about inflation over the next 12 months and its influence on wage and price levels. In short, looking from the inside out, the planners of accounting saw a great deal of the outside world. And some of this awareness percolated into the rest of the company.

But then, in the 1960s, financial planning underwent another refinement. Rather than relying on an educated head-office guess at next year's sales, many companies developed "bottom-up" planning. The planners went out to the people close to the action, managers throughout the organization, and asked (for instance) each district manager what he thought he would sell next year, two years from now, and even five years hence. The planners added up all the figures (changing some if they did not like the totals) and compiled the results into the "budget" or "forecast," or whatever it might be called.

From here it was only a small step to "management by objectives." If we were going to take the trouble of going all the way to the field and asking the district manager what he would sell next year, we might as well make him think very hard about the reply. Thus, if we agreed with his estimates, we would declare them to be his "target" figures. His performance would be checked and his rewards calculated on how well he chose and met his targets.

Now the forecast was an internal contract. Little outside information could break in, and all decisions emerged from the same introverted process. Planning, which had once been cast off from the "decision making" of the pragmatic line manager and relegated to a specialized intellectual realm, was now one of the principal vehicles for making decisions!

All through the 1950s and 1960s, the Shell Group faithfully took part in these developments. We finally reached our epitome of specialized planning with the launch in 1967 of the "Unified Planning Machinery"—the "planning system to end all planning systems." The UPM procedures, set out in a thick manual that all managers were supposed to follow, contained all of the elements of a state-of-the-art financial prediction system. There were target-setting and performance control procedures, to be administered going both up and down the hierarchy and applied inside each of the more than 100 countries in which the group operated. The estimates and predictions would gradually percolate from the local offices around the globe up into the coordinating units, which formed the matrix organization in the two central offices in London and the Hague. These meetings would finally culminate in a presentation to the Committee of Managing Directors and to the board, who would formally approve the capital budget and next year's operating plans.

This process continues today. Sometimes the time horizon looks out two years; other times, five. (The critical emphasis is in any case always on next year's figures.) Each year, the machinery is wound into action in June or July, in the operating companies. Each year, after countless meetings and reports, and an enormous amount of thought and effort, the board finally reaches its approval in December. Each year, the Unified Planning Machinery delivers its estimates of future activity, and each year, the group as a whole bases its investment decisions on those estimates.

There's only one problem. Whenever times are turbulent, and anticipating the future is the most critical, the Unified Planning Machinery is wrong. Dead wrong. It failed to foresee the spike in oil prices in the 1970s, when OPEC coalesced into a more powerful cartel. It failed to anticipate the collapse of oil prices in the mid-1980s, when the OPEC cartel devolved. And UPM failed to predict the restructuring of the oil business in the 1980s and 1990s, as the greater source of profits switched from one part of the business (production) to another part (downstream and marketing) and back again. Even during the 1960s, which were relatively quiet years for the oil business, those who looked could see this type of problem with UPM already emerging.

## Shell's Scenario Experience

Fortunately for Royal Dutch/Shell, it was also developing an alternative tool for looking at the future, alongside the Unified Planning Machinery. This technique, called "scenario planning," was well suited for building memories of the future. Unfortunately for a conventional manager, the scenario approach presupposes that the future is plural. Scenario planning requires managers to abandon the one-line approach, the assumption that there is only one predicted future to concern oneself with. In scenario planning, there is always more than one scenario.

Each scenario is simply an imaginative story about the future—a sketch of the "lot of life" as it could develop from the present moment into the future. The name was chosen and popularized by Herman Kahn, the well-known futurist from the Rand Corporation and the

Hudson Institute. (He borrowed the name from the movie industry; the original meaning of the word, as the *Oxford English Dictionary* defines it, is a " sketch of the plot of a play; giving particulars of the scenes, situations, etc."[4]) Kahn was best known for his scenarios about nuclear war, in which he advocated that people should "think about the unthinkable" so that, if nuclear war *did* become imminent, society would be less vulnerable and less likely to slide into a holocaust.

Scenario planning has been practiced in some form since the early 1960s, but even today, it remains surrounded by vagueness and an air of mystery. People are unsure whether it is a process for reaching better decisions, a way to know the future better, or a combination of both. Many scenarios, like science fiction stories, look at the future of mankind as a whole or the economics of an entire region; to a businessperson, it is not clear what to do with these. When trying to sell soap powder in Canada or manufacture power generators in Switzerland, the businessperson needs a translation of these grand, overarching developments into something closer to and more recognizable in his or her own world. The plot needs to be focused on its particular audience.

Learning to focus scenarios on a business purpose was in fact part of Shell's contribution to the practice. In the year 1968, soon after the introduction of UPM, an ad hoc study group within Shell undertook a study on "the year 2000." The impetus was the same predictive question that would later spark the long-term survivors study: How soon would the world run out of oil? And, if those resources were depleted, would that condemn oil companies to an unexciting, low-growth future? In short, as Shell people put it, "Is there life [for our company] after oil?"

The *Year 2000* study was professionally done and produced real business results in the Shell Group. A metal-producing company was bought; a 50 percent stake was taken in a nuclear venture and an internationally trading coal division was started. These outcomes were not all successful, and Shell retreated in the end from many of them. In retrospect, it could have been seen from the beginning that diversification would take place. It was implicit in the question: Is there life after oil? If you want the answer to be yes, then you must enter some other business. In the early 1970s, the only way to generate that business, at a scale appropriate for a major oil company, was to acquire or instigate it from the top, in a centralized move: diversification.

But the *Year 2000* study also had a second outcome. A new planning division was conceived, with a core group of some of Shell's more innovative people. These included Pierre Wack, Ted Newland, Peter Beck, and Napier Collyns—people who are now known for their writing and work on planning, even outside Shell. They were familiar with Herman Kahn's work, and they started to build on it, developing their own form of the scenario technique as a possible answer to two questions:

> How do we look 20 to 30 years ahead?
> How can we get people to discuss together the "unthinkable"?

Like Herman Kahn, the scenario planners tried to grasp the changing forces in the social values, technology, consumption patterns, political thinking, and financial structures of the world at large. But, unlike Kahn, Shell's scenario planners remained focused on the future of the oil industry. As Pierre Wack, the leader of the scenario team, never ceased to explain, "Scenarios must be *relevant*." To help businesspeople better understand what the future could mean, the plots had to play in the world of their own business. Only then would a manager see the relevance of global forces and possible futures. Only then would these stories help to raise the eyes toward the horizon.

In this sense, scenarios are neither a mystery nor a superior way of "planning." They are tools for foresight—discussions and documents whose purpose is not a prediction or a plan, but a change in the mindset of the people who use them. By telling stories about the future in the context of our own perceptions of the present, we open our eyes for developments which in the normal course of daily life are indeed "unthinkable." Relevant scenarios, brought down to the level of the individual player, help the manager and his or her colleagues scout the lay of the land and see a wider scenery. Scenarios bring new views and ideas about the landscape into the heads of managers, and they help managers learn to recognize new "unthinkable" aspects of the landscape even after the scenario exercise is over. As Pierre Wack liked to express it, "Good scenarios change the microcosms of management."

To accomplish this, it is not enough for the scenario writers to look out at the world from the narrow perspective of the company, as if from a window in the company's building. One has a rather limited view from most business edifices. Planners must go out into the wide world. Once out there, they have to look back at their company and ask themselves the question: What relevance could the driving forces that we see, externally, have for the more limited world of our own company and industry? This need for wider perspective explains the exotic list of sources of inspiration that Peter Schwartz (longstanding scenario planner and Royal Dutch/Shell scenario team leader during the mid-1980s) proposes in his book *The Art of the Long View*. Schwartz suggests that the budding futurist learn to look at the fringes. Talk to people "with whom you disagree deeply, but can talk amicably." Read widely, ranging far outside your immediate business interests (from design magazines to self-published youth "zines" to government journals, he suggests), but don't forget the *Economist*.[5]

From its beginnings in the early 1970s, the Shell planning group developed an extensive network of outside contacts who were chosen for their insights and understanding of what went on in the world at large. Pierre Wack called them his "Remarkable People." Historian Art Kleiner describes his method this way:

> [Wack] sought out acute observers with keen, unending curiosity. These people devoted themselves to *seeing:* to constant attention to the ways the world worked. . . . Sometimes, a remarkable person from outside Shell might stumble into a scenario presentation, as an Iranian physician did in the early 1970s, looking for stimulating conversation. . . . The two men became close friends. Each year Pierre would visit and ask how his perception had changed.[6]

The scenario planners tried to grasp what was changing in a wide variety of arenas: social values, technology, consumption patterns, political thinking, and international finance in the world at large. There was little duplication with the planning still done by Shell supply or finance people, who were looking only at oil-related developments. The new planners did not ignore oil and energy concerns, but they were looking for "driving forces," which might come from anywhere and ultimately work through to affect the world of energy and oil. They analyzed these forces to see whether, and how, the resulting changes might affect their own businesses. In short, scenarios provide tools through which the nonfashionable and weak signals may be picked up and considered, without overwhelming the managers who use them.

Scenarios also hone managers' judgment about the significance of those forces, by providing new ways to group and consider them. In the big, wide world in which Shell (or any company) operates, there are always many driving forces for change, interacting with each other in a bewildering blizzard of mutual causes and effects. To plot them all would lead to confusion and (probably) despair: no one could ever make sense of all this! This explains why well-crafted scenarios typically combine a number of forces together into a story that seems simple, but is actually quite sophisticated.

Spending time discussing a scenario allows managers to see long-term interactions—among, for instance, their own capital investment plans, the energy efficiency of consumers, and Middle Eastern politics. In the process, the managers develop a language in which they can later communicate among themselves about the subject, to arrive quickly at decisions. The scenario gives them a context for considering all of these forces—perhaps not comprehensively, in the manner of an academic dissertation, but dynamically. A story of a falling oil price can bring all of these forces vividly to life in the imagination, so that they linger in "memories of the future," in words that are understandable to colleagues.

In the interaction among driving forces, there is always a range of possible outcomes. Many listeners will ask, "What is the most probable outcome?" But the answer is: All of the possible interactions among the same set of driving forces in a complex system have equal probability of taking place. For that reason, several scenarios will have to be written: enough to condition managers to see past many of their blind spots. The number of scenarios is important. Too many scenarios confuse the manager. An uneven number gives the manager an unfortunate escape route; it's too easy to bypass the scenarios' implications by picking "the one in the middle," the compromise future that is seen as an alternative to the extremes. Two is probably a good number for scenario exercises; it forces the manager to make a choice between them and thus to think through the ramifications of both of them.

Once written, scenario stories are tested and quantified with the help of simulation models and (in the case of the Royal Dutch/Shell Group) the company's data banks on energy and economics. The quantification helps focus the scenarios, and it shows whether the stories are internally consistent. The end result is a series of consistent, plausible futures, which don't merely provoke thought. If they're successful, they should provoke surprise and even emotion. "I never realized this could happen to us," people might say.

Having a low number of scenarios inevitably means that the writing process is one of reduction. Conceivably, several thousand pages of interviews and studies might result from as many as two years of study and research. All of these reports have to be reduced to a booklet that can be read in a sitting. This means, preferably, a booklet of less than 70 pages. The person who writes the final draft of this booklet must be a good storyteller, with a nose for the main themes to be developed. The best-remembered scenarios, in fact, have some of the characteristics of fairy or folk tales.

Indeed, the mythological elements of the Hero's journey, as Joseph Campbell noted in his book *The Hero with a Thousand Faces*, seem to resonate fairly well for most modern businesspeople. The Departure, the Belly of the Whale, Initiation on the Road of Trials, and finally the Return (having earned the Freedom to Live) all have parallels in scenario stories. In my experience, some of the scenarios that were best understood and longest remembered by the Shell organization had elements of Joseph Campbell's description of the timeless Adventure:

> The mythological hero, setting forth from his hut or castle, is lured or voluntarily proceeds to the threshold of adventure. There he encounters a shadow presence that guards the passage. The hero may defeat this power and go alive into the kingdom of the dark . . . journeying through a world of unfamiliar forces, some of which severely threaten him. When he arrives at the nadir, he undergoes a supreme ordeal and gains his reward. The final work is that of the return . . . the hero re-

emerges from the kingdom of dread. The boon that he brings restores the world.[7]

We saw this theme, for instance, in Pierre Wack's scenario of the "Rapids" (an anticipation of the turbulence of the late 1970s) or Peter Schwartz's "The Next Wave" (an early glimpse of the global economy of the 1990s). In both of these worlds, the corporate hero had to conquer first the rapids of an economic recession or the threat of a world of low oil prices, before the boon (of microchip technology) would reward the hero and restore the world. Both scenarios helped to change the Shell corporate mind and opened our eyes for the gloomy messages of, respectively, a recession and a world of low prices. It was plausible that we could survive and even thrive through the crisis. On these occasions, the message was absorbed without the messenger (the planner) being shot. Such is the power of a strong, symbolic story!

In the telling (through presentations), the story line becomes stronger. Scenarios act as a signal-to-noise filter. The driving forces sharpen. The events depicted enter the mind with less background noise and thus with a stronger profile and clearer outlines.

The scenarios help managers see past their biases, but the bias of the scenario storyteller must also be taken into account. It is no surprise that, as creators of a work of art, different artists write different stories, based on their individual observations of the same realities. Some scenario writers have a message. They write "normative" scenarios: pictures that they believe will convince the listeners to join in creating or join in forestalling alternative worlds. Other scenario writers have a strongly developed framework for thinking about their world. They are so aware (for example) of the enormous influence of technology that they cannot easily imagine a world in which technology has *little* influence. Other scenario writers are more inductive; they tend to let the story evolve during the course of their one or two years of research, with little forethought about where the data may take them. They listen to the themes that emerge as different people talk about their observations. If they are successful, they produce a work of remarkable insight and power; if not, they produce a scattered mishmash of all the things they have heard.

Once the scenario is written, different people will present it to audiences in different ways. How well the scenario writers are heard depends, in part, on their skill and quality as presenters. Some scenario writers are preachers. They want their message to be heard. Some are almost mystical in their emphasis on the wide, overarching themes. And others focus on many nuances, to let the image emerge as if from the thousands of colored points in a Seurat painting.

Nearly always, if the scenario development has been conducted well, the results will be disturbing. The scenario presenter will have things to say that the line manager will experience as unwelcome intrusions in his or her business thinking. To be heard through a veil of emotional denial requires scenario writers with a high degree of acceptability in circles of line management. That was why all of the chief scenario team leaders at Shell—starting with Pierre Wack and Ted Newland, through all of their successors—were carefully screened by every member of Shell's Committee of Managing Directors. As a group, the CMD "endorsed" not only the scenario leaders, but also every new set of scenarios before they were published in the Shell community.

Endorsement did not mean that each and every one of the managing directors agreed with the contents of the scenarios. Quite the contrary, on several occasions. But they agreed that the major themes of the scenarios deserved to be kept in mind, however distasteful or improbable the details of these themes might seem to be. Endorsement would never have been forthcoming if the directors had not had an opportunity to convince themselves of the integrity and sound judgment of the principal scenario writers.

Public endorsement was not only necessary; it became official practice. Early in the 1970s, the CMD issued a planning rule: annual capital and operating budgets had to be defended against the background of the scenarios "*en vigeur.*" For those of us in line management, there was no way around it. We had to show that we had at least considered the possibilities that the scenarios had raised. If we wanted our budgets approved, we had to read the scenarios with great attention and make sure that we had our counterarguments ready.

This is a remarkable illustration of the power of corporate rules, if issued with wisdom and followed with self-discipline. The result was a widespread attentiveness to outside events that was so thorough it was hardly noticed after a while. It simply became "the way things are done around here" to consider the effects of external forces that might seem counterintuitive at first. Without this rule, it is a real possibility that, today, the Shell Group would still be a company with a one-track mind, blissfully unaware that the future is uncertain and different from a "preferred" one-line forecast.

Even so, endorsing and legislating attentiveness to the scenario process was not enough. There had to be a head of planning who could stand in for the line managers and represent their concerns and attitudes at every step of the scenario-creating process. In the 25 years since the group decided to set up its scenario planning outfit, it has never appointed a professional planner to head this activity. The six individuals who have been head or coordinator of Group Planning (including myself) had been line managers, mostly with a finance or exploration background.

Presumably, this helped to keep the activity rooted in the business. It also helped to infuse it with a little credibility. The colleagues of the chief planners' previous "line" incarnation were inclined to give him some benefit of the doubt, at least in the beginning. Even so, the role of chief planner was often that of an unwelcome messenger of bad news, a doomsayer. Most managers find it tiresome, at the moment when they are busy spending a few hundred million dollars buying a concession or extending a refinery, to stop and spend time "thinking the unthinkable." The planning coordinator's little capital of fraternal goodwill dissipates rather quickly in those circumstances. Perhaps this is the strongest argument for appointing line managers, rather than professional planners, to head the corporate planning activity. (But don't leave an ambitious young line manager in that post for too long, because it could kill a career. Any planner runs the risk, in the long run, of being seen as an irrelevant court jester, or a Rasputin whispering mysterious schemes in the managing directors' ears. Neither is an attractive career prospect!)

Hopefully, the foregoing paragraphs have demonstrated the dimensions of scenarios as tools and the tool-building nature of scenario practice. Since the early Shell experiences, there has been a growing interest in this new practice for corporate foresight. The first good books on the subject are now available to the public. Peter Schwartz's *The Art of the Long View*[8] explains how to conduct a scenario exercise. Kees van der Heijden's *Scenarios: The Art of Strategic Conversation*[9] is a solid handbook on the principles of scenario planning. Art Kleiner's *The Age of Heretics*[10] recounts how Herman Kahn, Pierre Wack, Ted Newland, and others developed the practice.

## The Bridge between Scenarios and Action

Ironically enough, a deemphasis on prediction seems to lead to accuracy about the future. It is remarkable how often the scenarios published at Shell over the years predicted important developments in the world around the Shell Group, often years ahead of time. The timing and the quantification of these events or trend breaks were not always right, but the scenarios were often quite clear about the results and implications of the change.

Shell's scenario makers rightfully claim that they recognized the future ahead of its time. They foresaw the energy crises of 1973 and 1979, the growth of energy conservation and the reduction of demand for oil, the evolution of the global environmental movement, even the breakup of the Soviet Union. Shell's management had the opportunity to take cognizance of important changes in the world, and it was early enough to make the decisions necessitated by these external changes. Many people would say that this gave the Shell Group an important competitive advantage.

Yet, in the early 1980s, both top management and planners felt uncomfortable with the scenario approach. We could see no discernible influence, from this advance knowledge, on the major decisions that had actually been taken during the previous decade.

Top management saw an expensive planning outfit which produced colorful stories, very useful for public relations, but too far removed from the real business. They remembered occasions when the planners had sketched a future that had not come to pass. They showed little awareness of the occasions when the planners had been "right." Top managers began to say that this planning effort should be "closer" to the real business.

The planners, certainly, were less harsh in their judgment, but they found it equally difficult to cite a convincing example of a decision that had been taken after a scenario had highlighted a critical change. In their defense, the planners maintained that scenarios were not supposed to work in such a crude and direct fashion. Instead, as noted earlier in this chapter, they argued that scenarios served to change the ways that managers saw and understood their world. Scenarios were designed to oblige managers to question their assumptions and reorganize their inner mental maps of reality

What did that mean in simple business terms? It meant that scenarios were supposed to make managers say, "Aha! Now I understand what's going on!"[11] As a result, the planners argued, decision makers would make decisions different than the ones they might have made otherwise.

However, how to achieve this "aha" experience in the minds of managers was not quite clear. This was seen as the real challenge of scenario analysis and clearly not solely dependent on the eloquence of the presentation and the beauty of the charts.

In short, we in Group Planning were facing a real enigma. We could see, in retrospect, that scenarios had a proven track record of reasonably reliable predictions, well ahead of time. But we could not offer the skeptics any demonstrable evidence that the Shell Group, as a whole, had changed its behavior or become more adaptive. There was at best a weak link between our advance knowledge and the actual business decisions that had been made during the previous decade.

Perhaps the issue was not scenarios at all, but the decision-making process that they were intended to influence. Could it be that corporate decision-making processes needed some improvement? And, if so, what was the real nature of decision making in the Shell Group—and elsewhere? We resolved to explore these issues at Group Planning. We would investigate whether the very act of decision making could be redesigned, to influence managers—and the company as a whole—to learn.

# 4

# Decision Making as a Learning Activity

IN RETROSPECT, PERHAPS I WAS TOO HASTY IN MY ENTHUSIASM when we first began to reflect on the decision-making process at Shell Group Planning in the mid-1980s. First, we had started to think about the role of planning in the company's decision-making processes. Phrases like "planning is a catalyst" came easily to our minds, working as we were in the oil and chemical industries. Then we developed the idea that "planning is learning." Only gradually did it dawn on us that decision making itself could be a learning process.

In retrospect, I can see that I came to this understanding quite naturally. In the previous decade, my two daughters had been of school age, and my attention had been directed to the subject of learning. I had read the work of John Holt,[1] and it had revived some of my old university interests in psychology. So I began to talk about "learning" and "accelerating learning," for the whole organization. We could gain, I argued, by speeding up the rate of that learning. But I was not always heard with approval. Organizations, I was told, do not learn. People learn.

Statements like these stem from a view of decision making, and another view of learning, that are embedded in the prevailing culture of

Royal Dutch/Shell and in society at large. These points of view are in-
herited from the practices and theories of academia and management.
The two activities, learning and decision making, are supposed to be
completely separate.

In academia, decision making is called a science. The student can
follow courses on the subject; books are written about it. The practitioners of this science, trained in the art of management, sit in their offices and follow the expert steps for making appropriate decisions.
There is no need to learn during the decision process; they have already
learned everything they need to know.

As for learning itself, according to the prevailing view, you (if you
are a manager, at least) are supposed to learn only during a particular
part of your life: the school years. This learning time is a time of fun,
without too much responsibility. Then you move into real life, into
work at a company where you apply your knowledge. Play stops and
hard reality takes over. You are paid for what you know. The more you
know (or have learned in school), the more you should earn. Education
is not a vehicle for expanding your capability, but simply a credential
for bettering your lot.

Having more knowledge may ultimately mean that you become a
leader. Then, at last, people will listen to you. They will be convinced
by your logical arguments and the superior array of facts at your disposal. If they still do not carry out your commands (assuming that you
have explained them clearly, reasonably, and calmly), it is probably because other people in the organization—wittingly or otherwise—put
barriers in the way. It is your job to have those removed. Leadership
has as little to do with learning as decision making does. Indeed, when
a leader says, "I learned something I didn't know before," it detracts
from his or her ability to appear certain and thus to inspire confidence.
A leader who learns is a leader who is unsure.

This attitude is a cartoon of intelligent human life. It portrays people as motorcars: you start at a service station (university) and fill up
your "brain tank" with knowledge. Then you use your intellectual fuel
to advance down life's highway. In this view, there is no need for institutions to make learning happen more effectively or on a larger scale.
All the knowledge of the company is already embedded in the heads
of its employees. Learning, except perhaps for a bit of "touch-up"

learning to stay abreast of new technologies, is assumed to be already covered.

This view is reflected in the way we recruit, remunerate, and promote people. There is no place at the top for an actor who seeks to anticipate outside events by (for example) bringing people together to look at developments that *might* turn into a crisis. There is no room for someone who admits that he or she does not have all the answers. The idea that the company itself could do some learning of its own does not enter into anyone's thinking.

## The Reality of Decision Making

In the 1980s, as we studied the core intellectual activity of the organization around us, we began to reject the prevailing hypothesis. Once attuned, I could easily see for myself that decision making was a *learning* process. It was, in fact, hardly individual at all. It was primarily a social process, simple, unheroic, and unscientific.

After all, what happens in decision-making meetings? People talk. Analytical techniques, such as net present value, earning power calculations, and optimization models, may be included in the preparation of information for the meetings. But in themselves these are barren soil for decisions. Decisions grow in the topsoil of formal and informal conversation—sometimes structured (as in board meetings and the budget process), sometimes technical (devoted to implementation of specific plans or practices), and sometimes ad hoc.

Suppose that you and I are part of a team, holding meetings to make a decision. Look closely at what happens during such a meeting. We talk. Ideally, we talk freely and openly. If we have any hope of reaching a decision, we know the meeting can't be dominated by one person—certainly not by the boss. We know that nobody in the room has the solution at hand. We will have to struggle together to find an answer to a situation that concerns us all. If the meeting is to be effective, therefore, none of us can lose patience with the thought processes of our colleagues. We cannot throw our weight around or stand on our stripes.

However, even if our meetings are not well organized and well managed, they are still conducted through conversation. This process of conversation goes through four stages.[2] They can be described best, I believe, in cybernetic terms:

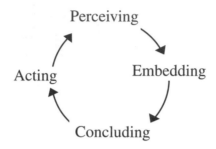

Perceiving

Acting                    Embedding

Concluding

1. **Perceiving.** A meeting is called because somebody has seen or heard of an event or phenomenon that is outside the normal course of business. Sales may have slipped, a government may have changed political color, or the competition may be offering a new product. People say, "We better start figuring out what it means to us!" In short, the stage of *developing a mental model*—an internal interpretation, coloring the way we look at that new event—has begun.

2. **Embedding.** Now we spend most of our time explaining to each other "how we see the problem." We try to understand its relationship to our known business world and to embed the change within our previous understandings. If our team is sufficiently diverse—with some technical participants, some from finance, some marketers, and some human relations people—we can gradually build a multifaceted picture of the situation. We invent language to "label" the modules of the model that we are beginning to share. We give birth to company jargon—shorthand expressions for parts of the understanding of the situation on which we now agree. We are *externalizing and calibrating our mental models* so that we may reach a coherent decision together.

3. **Concluding.** Gradually, shared understanding leads to plans for action. Somebody is bound to ask, "Now, what would happen, if . . . ?" From that moment on, the meeting becomes

even more disordered, and yet more productive. We talk through the "what if?" consequences of our options and potential actions. It is as if our shared understanding has become a model on the table before us, and we experiment with various conclusions. "What if we launched a new product? Or changed the packaging? Or switched prices?" You could arguably see this phase as *simulating a model* of the situation by running imaginary iterations of our decision.

4. **Acting.** Finally, we are ready for implementation and action. The only relevance of the decision making process resides in the action that results from it. However, we design the action, as best we can, to keep track of its effects, monitoring and evaluating the process. How do we know it will be a success? What can we do to be more certain of our observations? We are like scientists, *running a model,* making our ideas real so that we may perceive the effects . . .

. . . and the cycle begins all over again.

As it happens, these four elements—perceiving, embedding, concluding, and acting—are seen by various psychologists as the defining elements of learning. Whether they are managed effectively or not doesn't matter. *Every act of decision making is a learning process.*

## Learning by Accommodation

Based on his studies of children's' development, the Swiss education theorist Jean Piaget has proposed that there are two types of learning: assimilation and accommodation.[3]

*Learning by assimilation* means taking in information for which the learner already has structures in place to recognize and give meaning to the signal. (As David Ingvar would say, the learner already has a "memory of the past or the future" with which this information fits.) The learner can perceive, digest, and act on this information easily—in the way that a student, having looked up something in a textbook, can use it to answer a test question or an artisan can look up a technique and use it on the project.

In companies, most information used in operational decisions fits this category. For example, bank management instantly recognizes the signal of an important increase in the interest rate. The bank has all the procedures and structures in place to give meaning to the signal. The institution, at all levels, is ready to digest it—to come to conclusions and to act on it in decisions about deposits, loan transactions, money market operations, or any other bank business.

This is the activity most people have in mind when they think of learning—being exposed to facts and assimilating them intellectually. In this activity, there are ready-made ideas and structures that fit the situation. These ideas can be transmitted from one individual to another. This is the learning activity of the traditional lecture hall or classroom; it is so prevalent that many of us are conditioned to equate *learning* with *teaching*.

In companies, the closest one gets to teaching is when an expert or a consultant stands up in a management meeting and doles out his or her wisdom. This teaching is not the dominant method for training in companies. That's just as well—it shows that in companies, when performance counts, people recognize that teaching is an ineffective route to learning.

The other type of learning, as Piaget puts it, is *learning by accommodation*. In this type of learning, you undergo an internal structural change in your beliefs, ideas, and attitudes. When we learn by assimilation, says Piaget, the lectures and books of conventional school learning are sufficient. But learning by accommodation requires much more. It is an experiential process by which you adapt to a changing world through in-depth trials in which you participate fully, with all your intellect and heart, not knowing what the final result will be, but knowing that you will be different when you come out the other end. This interrelationship with the environment actually makes you grow, survive, and develop your potential.

Someone who undergoes a course of military training, for example, will no longer think or act the same way as before; the same is true for someone who goes through the rigors of in-depth professional school.

Corporations also have a form of learning by accommodation—at least, successful companies do. As we saw in the previous two chapters, long-lived companies find ways to respond to signals of change in the business environment, by changing their own internal structure. The same important increase in the interest rate, which the bank manager takes in stride, has a very different meaning for a heavily geared real estate company. It should lead the latter to changes in its internal structure. It should renegotiate its loans, get rid of part of its project portfolio, delay or change the nature of individual projects, try to find a partner, or reorient its workforce.

All of these forms of learning, in the end, are successful precisely because they are embedded in decision making. True decisions—in which a new understanding is reached and an action is taken—are all, in themselves, examples of learning by accommodation.

## The Problems with Conventional Learning

If decision making is learning, then *all companies learn all the time.* There is no need to "build" a learning organization. You already *have* a learning organization.

But the traditional time-honored ways in which most companies accomplish this learning are inadequate. The endless cycle of meetings and discussions have some distinct disadvantages.

- **They are slow.** In one Shell study, we measured the speed of decision making when the decisions involved a change in the internal structure of the company—shifting the product range, closing a manufacturing gate, or redesigning the organization. Such decisions often took 18 months between reception of the signal and implementation of the change. In some cases, it took five years or more between an item's appearing on the agenda for the first time and the final implementation of the required internal change.

  Being slow is especially dangerous in a world of frequent oscillations. We run the risk of reacting to the last disturbance, of "fight ing the last war," when the next one is already coming around the corner.

* **They close options.** Discussions on new business opportunities or painful decisions on cutting parts of the business always involve reallocation of resources. For example, if the company contemplates the closure of a manufacturing site, or its move to another country, the managers concerned feel threatened or believe genuinely that they are asked to make a sacrifice. This brings elements of negotiation into the decision-making process. Negotiations, normally, can only have one outcome: the negotiated or hierarchically imposed solution. This outcome becomes the one option for which the company makes a single time path into the future. It becomes "the plan," or "the strategy," and other options are never explored.

* **They depend on learning by experience, instead of by simulation.** This means that normal management requires constant experimentation with reality. British Airways would never allow pilots to fly a 747 without making them spend considerable time in a flight simulator. A pilot does not learn to fly an airplane by experimentation with a real plane full of passengers. Yet we find it acceptable to let managers "fly" their companies by trial and error. Unfortunately, there are as many human fates linked to the decisions of a manager as there are linked to the decisions of the BA pilot.

* **They breed fear.** When we are asked to discuss an important decision, in which fundamental change is involved, our minds tend to race ahead to think of the consequences. Fear of the risks begins to permeate the thought processes. It cramps our imagination; imaginative or adventurous options are often not seriously considered.

As Piaget might put it, the preferred solution (in a fearful situation) becomes that of assimilation, rather than real change. Managers continue to hope that the original distortion will be only a temporary aberration. They make decisions that might include cutting costs, cutting capital expenditures, cutting recruitment, or reducing the quality specifications of the products. (Please note that these decisions are not *always* problematic. They are perfectly good decisions if they are made because the company has a poor position vis-à-vis its competitors, is overcapitalized, has too many people, or suffers from some other fundamental weakness. But if these decisions are made as a quick reaction to a change in the outside world—for example, to a drop in total demand—then they represent a solution of assimilation where accommodation would be required.)

Decisions based on learning by assimilation can have dangerous outcomes. If, indeed, there is a fundamental change in the world outside, and managers sit there reassuring themselves, "Yes, it is a change, but it will return to normal and then we'll be leaner and meaner," then the risks are mounting rapidly. If prolonged, assimilation weakens internal systems. Cash flow reduces. Employees walk away; so do customers. At some stage, so do shareholders. If the original distortion was not an aberration, and it does not go away, then the company will slide into a crisis with its internal systems weakened.

Fear also creates a preference for the repetition of previous success formulas. "This reminds me of the situation we encountered 20 years ago," someone is bound to say. He or she goes on to describe the solution that worked then. The sigh of relief is audible: "If it worked then, it may work now!"

History does, in fact, repeat itself—but never in quite the same way. A 2 or 3 percent deviation in the conditions from the previous time to this time can make the difference between a good decision and a mediocre one.

In short, the natural learning process tends to limit the number of options—and it is slow. The speed, openness, inventiveness, and courage of our learning efforts must all be improved for our organization to survive.

The question before us, then, is: How can we improve the existing decision-making process? How can we accelerate and fortify the learning that already occurs?

## Learning to Play, and Playing to Learn[4]

My search for better modes of learning led me to the writing of several noted educational researchers. The three sources whose work helped most critically were British psychologist D. W. Winnicott *(Playing and Reality)* from the Tavistock Institute, American teacher/writer John

Holt *(How Children Learn)*, and the Media Lab's Seymour Papert *(Mindstorms: Children, Computers, and Powerful Ideas)*, based at the Massachusetts Institute of Technology.[5]

All three writers wrote primarily about classrooms and children, but reading their books with companies in mind, one is struck by the similarities. Classroom situations are easily turned into boardroom situations, as we discovered before long in Shell's Group Planning.

All three writers had essentially the same theme: the essence of learning is discovery through play. A decision-making process that accelerated learning could do so only by making skillful use of playing.

The psychiatrists of the Tavistock Institute had known this since the mid-1940s. They had been in charge of one of the most massive training and learning efforts of this century—the preparation of the Allied armies for the invasion of France in 1943. After the war, they formed the institute to continue their efforts. From their pioneering work, we get a better idea of what "play" really is and how it enhances the acquisition of knowledge among individuals or groups.

D. W. Winnicott first published his book *Playing and Reality* in 1971. In it, he coined the idea of a "transitional object." Play, he reasoned, is always conducted with a thing in hand: a toy. Girls play with dolls, boys with Lego sets, and toddlers of both sexes with Fisher-Price toys.

Playing with toys is very different from playing a game or playing in a sport. There is no way to win. The player is simply experimenting with an object that in some way represents reality. This brought home the difference between play and games. Play is experimenting with a toy that the player accepts as representing his or her reality. This makes the toy a representation of the real world with which the learner can experiment without having to fear the consequences. Underneath all the fun there is a very serious purpose: playing with one's reality allows one to understand more of the world we live in. *To play is to learn.*

Winnicott called these toys "transitional objects," because they help the child to *transit* from one phase in life to the next—from one level of understanding of the world to another. A girl, for example, invests a doll with a part of her reality. In her mind, the doll is her little brother or her friend. She experiments (plays) with it. The doll being only a toy, she can do so without having to fear the consequences. She can mutilate it and find out that particular actions do indeed lead to mutilation. She can toss or drop it, in ways her mother would never allow her to do with her real-life baby brother. In so playing, the girl acquires knowledge about relationships and about cause and effect. She learns to begin acting in real life at a higher level of development.

Businesspeople do something quite similar. When Shell (or any other oil company) develops a new oilfield in the North Sea, and a new oil drilling platform must be built, we do not experiment with reality! We will not build the structure, put it in 100 meters' depth of seawater, and see what happens. Instead, we build a scale model, which we put in a model of the seabed. Then we experiment with such scale models, sometimes for years on end. We subject our "toy" to all imaginable forces of waves and wind and time, to see what would likely happen. Then, and only then, we build the real thing.

Similarly, at a chemical company developing a new process, models will be made and experimented with for months—at the scale of the lab bench, in a pilot plant, and sometimes at a suboptimal production facility, before the final design is constructed. The same is true for a dike built in Holland, a massive dam—or any technical situation where we do not want accidents or victims.

The military, for which every error is a matter of life and death, rarely moves without having played endless "war games." Many of the operations in the Gulf War of 1991, along with the entire logistical supply chain, had been played out in computer simulations before the moves were made in reality. Similarly, in business, whenever the risks are great, we do not experiment with reality. We go through a protracted phase of experimenting with a model, a representation of reality, before we enter "real" life. Even spreadsheet programs are "toys," in this sense; managers can simulate major financial decisions, trying different versions of reality, before risking great sums of money in real life.

All of these examples should make one thing clear. We know extremely well in business that play is the best method of learning. That's why it never ceases to amaze me that, in most business *decision making,* "play" is not even considered as a vehicle for learning. Instead of simulating reality, we "learn from experience"—we experiment with reality itself.

We perceive a problem. We put it on the agenda of the next meeting. Come the day of the meeting, we do everything at once: understand what this agenda item is about, think about what might happen in the future around this subject, dream up an action to be taken, and launch its implementation. We do all this, preferably in one meeting, with two more items to go through before the two key people in the corner have to leave in a hurry to catch their planes.

This Rambo style of management is quite pervasive. It is mostly adequate, though not ideal, for operational decisions—where knowledge and priorities fit in harmony with the outside world. A bank reacting to an increase of interest levels, or a wealthy company making comparatively small investment decisions, can afford to make some decisions this way. However, heroic decision making becomes a high-risk gamble in unhealthy, persistent business situations where the only way out is an adaptation: closing a factory, a new direction for the research program, aborting a product launch.

We should therefore not be surprised that so many fatal mistakes are made in the change management of companies, or that so many managers have so little time to think because they are constantly engaged in firefighting. To me, this prevalence of mishap is a strong argument for running our companies with the same low tolerance for error in management that we currently employ in the more technical parts of the business. As many, if not more, human fates ride on the quality of management's decisions in a takeover, merger, plant closing, or product change as there are at risk on a North Sea platform or inside a Boeing 747. A marketing manager in even a relatively small company, such as Shell Kenya, influences many more people through his or her decisions than an airplane pilot with 350 passengers in a 747 aircraft. We should not be so willing to take more risks in nontechnical work simply because the results of our errors are less immediately violent.

## Building the Manager's Lego Set

Peter Schwartz, the head of the Shell scenario team during the 1980s, tells the story of how he was walking down the street in Palo Alto, the California university town. Suddenly, a stranger crossed the street and walked up to him.

"How's the future?" the stranger said. When Peter looked blankly at him, the stranger said, "You're Peter Schwartz, right? You write about the future, right? You're interested in computers and kids, aren't you? You ought to read a book called *Mindstorms* by Seymour Papert. You'd really like it."[6]

The stranger walked away, and Peter crossed the street (in Palo Alto, all you have to do is cross the street and you're in a bookshop) and bought a copy. Then he brought it back to Shell, where it gave us the next step in developing transitional objects for managers.

Papert was using the personal computer, which was still only a few years old at that time, as a transitional object for learning by children. Using LOGO, a computer language that Papert had helped invent, children could program a mechanical "turtle" (or a turtle on the screen) to move in various directions or to draw patterns. The world of turtles became, as Papert called it, a "microworld," which in turn helped children learn about the real world. The experience of LOGO programming was as close to pure play as one might imagine. For example, by controlling the turtle's motion, using commands to set position and velocity, the children developed a visceral, in-depth, "accommodated" (in Piagetian terms) understanding of Newtonian physics concepts such as the laws of motion. It was very easy to read Seymour Papert and see his microworlds as another form of transitional object.

From Papert's work, we concluded that we could put a representation of reality into a computer, and use that "play" dynamic to build depth of understanding among the Shell managers. We resolved to experiment. We brought in a computer scientist, a young university graduate, who developed a model of the oil supply chain.

Unfortunately, the model was quite simplistic. Managers turned on their computer screens, looked at it briefly, and put it aside. We learned a valuable lesson: Managers are much less pliable than children. Children have an immense capacity for imaginative substitution: they can invest their reality in almost any object and then play with it. But we seem to lose that capability with age; as adults, we only want to play with "toys" that meet reality halfway and are representative enough to be recognized as reality.

So we tried to put the managers' multidimensional world onto a two-dimensional computer screen. We thus found ourselves dealing with the problem of mapping—the same problem that cartographers have when they must express the complex reality of a country with only the dimensions of printed ink on paper. To solve a mapping problem in cartography, one needs to develop a simple, consistent set of symbols: black lines for railroads, red lines for highways, and blue lines for rivers, for example. We needed a similarly simple set of symbols with which to map business problems.

When Pierre Wack heard about this stage of our quest, he said, "Why don't you talk to Jay Forrester?" Under the name of System Dynamics, the MIT management professor Jay Forrester had developed a small set of simple symbols, built into a computer programming language, that was perfectly capable of mapping any business situation. When we visited Forrester at MIT, it became clear that his programming language, then called DYNAMO, was well suited for building models with the requisite complexity.

Unfortunately, computer modeling was so complex that there was no accessible real-time modeling available. Model making required teams of highly trained specialists, who needed months to make the model run, and by the time they came back, the situation had changed and the model no longer represented reality for the managers. We spent months trying to find a computer modeling system that we could use for real-time models: models programmed in the presence of the managers' group, incorporating their ideas and perceptions, to overcome their mistrust. Anything built outside their presence was regarded as a "black box"—put one answer in, get another out, and put it away. There was nothing compelling about it, and they didn't want to play.

Building a DYNAMO model also required months; but one of Forrester's graduate students, Barry Richmond, had begun to create a new piece of software called Stella. Richmond said that it was 100 times more effective than DYNAMO, and we at Shell were inclined to agree with him.

With Stella (later known as iThink[7]), we could build microworlds of our own business[8]—computer environments that showed, for example, the key variables in an oil supply chain (such as, for example, "Producer Price" and "Consumer Demand"), with their interrelationships defined as formulas that fit the way they interacted in reality. We could enter decisions that a manager might make (such as increasing certain types of supply allocations) and see how the results might shift over the course of months or years. And, as our understanding of the real supply chain improved, we could make changes in the model, to make it conform in ever-more-sophisticated ways to the reality around us. Here, at last, was modeling software that could be managed in real time.

System Dynamics turned out to be ideal for bringing forth the mental maps that we had sought to influence with scenarios. We would bring in managers to help articulate their business problems and cast them into the specifications of the computer software. Forrester and his colleagues of the System Dynamics group had developed a few simple symbols that permit the modeler to draw complicated business situations: arrows for lines of influence, squares for "stocks" of various types of capacities (the amount of oil held in our tanks, the level of current staff), circles for "flows" that governed the rate of change (the sales rates or rate of hiring), and feedback loops that suggested how a part of a system would either continue to accelerate its growth or move toward equilibrium.

Heretofore, the computer models that Shell managers knew (and usually deeply distrusted) were the linear models of physical situations like a refinery or a transport fleet. They had been used to calculate refinery optimizations and the like. But *these* models were different. Based on nonlinear equations, they described the evolving causal relationships embedded in complex business situations as they took place over time. One model, set up for the management team, demonstrated the value of establishing a comprehensive in-house oil commodities trading floor. Another model helped the management of a small biotechnology firm in the Shell Group chart their strategy options. A new automotive retail policy was developed in the Netherlands, as was a new natural gas strategy after the oil price falls of 1986.

What difference did the models make? We set out to answer that question. Because one cannot measure quality of decisions, we decided we would measure speed: How long did it take to get from the *perception* of a changed external reality to the *implementation* of a fundamental shift of operation? When we measured, we tended to find that the process of learning had accelerated by a factor of two or three; it was now two or three times as fast to implement a new internal system. The shift to a full, comprehensive trading floor, for example, was a response to changes that had taken place in the international oil market. The vertical integration that had held sway for 40 years, under pressure from nationalizations in the Arab world, was disintegrating fast. There had been spot markets in oil trading before, but oil companies did not immediately recognize their need to shift their managerial approach: from optimizing the flow of oil *within the company only* to being willing to say, "Every drop of oil that I have is in principle for sale— not just to our own companies, but to anyone."

Shell was not the first company to make this shift; British Petroleum set up a full-scale in-house oil trading floor well before we did. Nonetheless, Shell made the switch well in time for our own survival. This was abetted by a Stella model, with which top managers "played" during the early 1980s. Since they were responsible for the decision, the learning of Shell as a company depended on their perceptions. Thus, at the moment they recognized the shifting environment, the institution had perceived a shift. From that moment, Shell reoriented itself to create a trading floor and to develop the necessary support for the floor. It took us only six to seven months. Within the following year or two, the amount of oil traded in that system rose to become 40 to 50 times as much oil as actually, physically, moved through the real system of refineries and tankers. In the past, similar decisions had taken 18 months or more.

## What Computers Couldn't Do

Despite these successes, we began to see, during the late 1980s, that system dynamics models were not a panacea. They were particularly problematic in the first phase of every team learning exercise: the capture of the mental models of the individual team members.

There were three parts to this task: (1) capturing the (often-unarticulated) understanding that a group of managers held about their world; (2) mapping this understanding in a visual, two-dimensional form on the computer screen; and (3) creating the computer model in real time, with the managers present. When all three steps came together, managers could see with their own eyes that the symbols on the screen were commensurate with the views they had expressed in words.

But the process often didn't come together. More often than not, when we began to put two or three managers' explanations together into the same model, calibrated against one another, we saw a reversal to the old, suspicious attitudes about computer "black boxes." Those meetings were fiascoes. It would be impossible to get the group of managers to start *playing*. Instead of simulating their experiences and learning about external reality, they became critics of the model. They passed hours querying its assumptions, pointing out omissions, criticizing the modeling techniques—anything but learning about their environment!

I often wondered, in those days, why children had so much more imagination than results. They were prepared to play with toys that weren't exact representations of reality; they knew they could learn from those toys. Grown-up managers wanted the model to resemble not just reality, but *their own assumptions about the external reality.* If in doubt, they would refuse to play.

Other companies have had similar experiences. Often, the question "Whose model is it?" takes precedence over the question "What is this model saying?" Peter Senge and some of his MIT colleagues, for example, developed a set of models of the claims adjustment processes for the Hanover Insurance Company in Worcester, Massachusetts. I have seen some of the Hanover people play it. An element of competition immediately creeps into the play situation: learning is only a by-product. They have little concern for understanding the situation described by the simulation. Their concern is "How can I master the game, to score more points than the boss?" They want to finesse the game instead of learning what the game can teach them.

Clearly, the computer itself was getting in the way of our primary purpose: understanding the system. We were asking managers to pile on several unfamiliar processes in one meeting. First, they had to talk together about their assumptions, breaking the hallowed traditions of meeting conduct in a corporation. Second, they had to look at symbols on a computer screen, put there much too quickly by some young computer expert. And, third, they had to put up with the on-screen spaghetti and expect that this was a reliable representation of the discussion. We were asking too much.

So we eliminated the computer. Instead, we moved to a distinctly low-tech technique: noting our ideas on magnetic, colored hexagons, which are placed on a whiteboard so that everyone can see what is written on them. We then cluster and rearrange the hexagons at will to show related concepts or connections between ideas.[9] There are other "soft mapping" techniques; indeed, a great deal of interesting group dynamics research is going on in the UK in this area of soft modeling and cognitive mapping.

Even teams of very senior managers react positively to soft modeling techniques like the hexagons, particularly at the early stages of mapping a team's mental models.[10] We have found it useful to move from there to a second phase, in which the team's concepts are converted into a systems model. The computer models give the team its only way to discover what Jay Forrester calls the "counter-intuitive consequences" of their actions—the long-term, unanticipated, far-flung results of internal policies and options. The computer reveals the underlying relationships and dynamics of a business situation in a far superior way to simple soft modeling. But the managers need not become computer scientists in the process. One does not learn how to ride a bicycle by designing one; and a management team learns about its environment, not by designing the computer representation, but by using it.

Accepting this view means facing the difficulty of converting the shared hexagon map (or a team's causal loop diagram, as described in *The Fifth Discipline Fieldbook*)[11] into a fully quantified computer model. There is a long way to go before this problem is solved. Management teams, especially senior ones, grow impatient with this process; they do not want to sit there while their perceptions are quantified into the computer model. Thus the temptation always exists to dismiss the team and hand over the flipcharts and hexagons to a computer modeler, who will put the project together in a back-room office. Neither managers nor computer modelers seem to wish for anything better.

This temptation should be resisted. Any model emerging from the modeler's back-room office runs an unacceptably high risk of being rejected by the team. The modeler simply doesn't know what they know; the modeler can't make the model represent their understanding of their reality. I believe that the solution to this problem ultimately lies in designing a computer language similar to Seymour Papert's LOGO. If a computer language can be created simple enough to allow six-year-olds to design their own micro worlds, it ought to be possible to create a language for managers.

## Why Don't We Play All the Time in Business?

I hope I have shown, in this chapter, how the decision-making process is in fact a learning process in any company and that there are ways to improve the speed, if not the quality, of the decisions. The more in-depth the simulation, and the more that "play" triggers the imagination and learning, the more effective the decision-making process seems to be. In companies that attempt large-scale internal change, this is particularly true. Decisions cannot be made in the old authoritarian manner. They need interaction, intuitive reflection, and the fostering of collaborative mental models. They need play. They need learning.

Despite its reasonable nature, this is a hard message for managers to hear. It goes against the traditional way in which most people look at their career position. They do not think about their job in terms of learning. Intellectually, they may agree, but they still feel that their leadership depends on their "knowing"—their ability to project self-assured confidence in their own information. The corollary notion, that "the best way to learn is through play," makes the message even less palatable.

This was certainly the case in the mid-1980s, when I had been planning coordinator for about five years. I still did not find it easy to talk to my colleagues about decision making as a learning process, or about learning as "play." Finally, I dared give a talk about the subject at a Shell planners' conference, in 1986, in the distant village of Banff, Canada. That talk was well received, but it was still not easy to discuss the subject at top management levels in London or The Hague.

Even the phrase "I learned" was inadmissible in many Shell circles—which made it very difficult for people to enter into the kind of colloquy that would help us improve our decisions. To have to "learn" something meant you didn't know it in the first place, and (particularly for those of us who came of age in the 1950s), it was considered much better to lie and give an answer—any answer—than to admit you don't know. This attitude is still ingrained in many companies—sometimes deeply ingrained.

In the end, one of my colleagues, Napier Collyns, advised me that I would find a more attentive audience if I talked "from the outside in." At his suggestion, I wrote a *Harvard Business Review* article, published in 1988 under the title "Planning as Learning." The article stayed prudently in the area of planning and only touched obliquely on the subjects of this book: decision making and the nature of companies. And it worked! It was now possible to hear the word *learn* in speeches from senior managers at Shell, and to develop more experimental approaches to management decisions. Since then, the debate in the Shell Group has made important steps forward, and gradually there is a wider application in more fields of the theories and practice of institutional learning.

Ultimately, if companies do not embrace the hypothesis of "accelerating learning" and the concept of "play," they will suffer the serious, long-term effect of learning more slowly than their competitors. Thus the living company needs to find a way to cope with inbred resistance to seeming "incorrect." Something must be done to make the members of the company feel secure in the company's identity, so that they can reveal themselves safely and speak up with impunity. These are matters that move beyond learning; they have to do with building a coherent identity.

# PERSONA (IDENTITY)

# 5

# Only Living Beings Learn

WITH THE CONCEPT OF "PLAY" UNDERSTOOD, WE BEGIN TO SEE how companies can learn beyond the learning of individual managers. Imagine that you have a team embarked on a steady regime of "play" within a company. People regularly join the team or leave it to pursue other projects, so that, by the end of three or four years, no original team members are left. Yet the *team's* capabilities continue to improve. The caliber of projects that the team takes on continues to improve, because each new team member is brought along to experience the same quality of learning.

Now imagine that there are similar teams throughout this company. People still join and leave the company, but the caliber of learning continues because the practice of play is institutionalized. Outsiders, watching the company's financial and social results, are moved to exclaim, "It's amazing how this company has developed! It is far more capable, and far more resilient, than it used to be!"

What is the entity they are talking about? Is it the set of teams that are learning? Is it simply the sum of the managers who are active in the company? Or is this greater capability embodied in the company's factories, oilfields, ships, and trucks? In other words, does the balance sheet reflect the company's ability to develop its capabilities? Why is the company worth more or less than it was a decade ago? Is this change inherent in the assets on the balance sheet? Is it possible that a bundle of assets can learn?

Assets are just dead objects. They have nothing to do with the innate spirit that moves and propels a company. Nor is a company just a bundle of individuals, or a combination of assets and individuals. We have already seen how companies can survive the loss of both assets and individuals, and more, and still keep their essential nature intact. Thus it is impossible to talk about organizational learning without trying to think about every company as a living being. But this is an unusual line of thought. We expect living beings to have cells and bodies; to be born, die, and reproduce; to take in nutrients and give off waste. Do corporations, with their abstract, legally created bodies, do anything of the sort?

If a company is a living being, what is that being like?

These questions became important to me around 1971. That was the year that I reached a personal turning point—a moment of intense soul searching that, in retrospect, defined the rest of my working life and career.

I had just been appointed to be a director of Shell Brazil. But it was an inauspicious time to be placed in the top management of a major oil company in South America. Two years after I came to Brazil, the world was in the throes of the oil crisis. Embargoes came into effect against many countries. Supply was curtailed. Long lines of cars with frustrated drivers lined up at the forecourts of service stations—primarily in the United States and Europe, but also elsewhere in the world.

At that moment in history, Brazil was doing relatively well. The country was in the middle of "the Brazilian miracle": 15 years of uninterrupted economic growth. This growth required lots of oil, which had to be imported. But Brazil's government-owned oil company, Petrobras, had been canny. It had acted quickly to set up supply lines. Since the oil kept coming, the economy kept growing, and Brazil's exports continued to pay for the ever-increasing price of oil imports.

Nonetheless, the oil crisis helped rekindle Brazil's nationalistic fires, always easy to bring to flame. Years before, under the slogan "O petroleo è nosso" ("The oil is ours"), the petroleum industry had been all but monopolized in government hands. Exploration and production, as well as refining and transport, of oil within Brazil were handled exclusively by Petrobras. Private companies (like Shell) were grudgingly permitted to bring in oil imports and to retail them in the domestic market. But now Petrobras had beaten the oil companies at the supply game; it had succeeded, where they had failed, to bring in the oil the country needed for its growth.

Hence, a chorus of voices emerged, asking to remove the foreign companies from their last foothold in oil retailing. Petrobras could do better. Besides Brazilian nationalism, the chorus drew on an increasingly strident worldwide theme. In the court of public opinion, multinational corporations were the culprits responsible for the "outrage" of the oil crisis. Individuals around the world in those days were asserting their rights against large-scale universities, armies, governments, and multinational corporations. Small had been declared beautiful. From the point of view of this rhetoric, it was easy to see that large global oil companies, bigger than many nations, had power that eclipsed mere sovereign control. They used (or, rather, abused) their power, creating artificial shortages for their own egoistic purposes and manipulating the markets to increase their already-obscene profits. Individuals were thus deprived (said the critics) of the natural right to move around in a motorcar whenever one wished.

You could hear such remarks, at that time, coming from the mouths of politicians, in reports in the press, in United Nations communiqués, and even in the voices of some of my friends and acquaintances. The scorn hit me hard. I had already been working more than 20 years, by then, for one of these multinational oil companies. My father had worked for the same company. Where I came from, getting employment in such a solid, large-scale organization had always been an occasion for celebration, not calumny. Moreover, I had worked for Royal Dutch/Shell in Europe, the Middle East, Africa, and now South America. I had come to know hundreds of my colleagues at nearly all levels of the hierarchy. I did not recognize myself or my colleagues in the descriptions the press and politicians were giving.

I could, to be sure, write off many of the critical comments as cynically self-serving political statements. But there was no doubting the depth, or the sincerity, of the emotions people expressed.

My other colleagues, who worked in these maligned multinational institutions, felt similarly startled, hurt, and misunderstood. From childhood onward, we had joined a wide variety of institutions: churches, clubs, trade unions, professional organizations, and, finally, companies. Why would we be acceptable as members of a church or a club, but socially suspect because we worked in a large company?

Before long, however, we realized we had nothing to fear. We could protect ourselves by keeping silent and keeping the *company* below the parapet of public attention. The attacks were all focused on the *company*, not on the individuals involved in it. The company was seen (and caricatured) as a unit in its own right, with its own purposes and its own characteristics. Outsiders could not fathom its intentions and machinations—particularly when a company like Shell had foreign roots, seemingly not subject to the control of the national society (of Brazil, in this case). To outsiders, a company like Shell had the mysterious power of making its employees do things which those individuals would never do acting in their own right.

It all added up to an image of Shell as a sort of giant phantom in a forest—difficult to see, with no specific contours, but with enormous, uncontrolled, undefined powers that might well do us harm. Moreover, it was a silent phantom. The multinational entity told no story about itself. Outsiders could only guess why it existed, what it did for a living, why it came to Brazil, and how the world would be different if the company did not exist at all.[1]

Many managers at Shell, and at other multinational companies, ignored this outsider's perspective; they were too busy managing the company, perhaps, to pay attention to the rantings of politicians and the press. From my Brazilian perspective, however, it was impossible to ignore. It made me wonder whether the stereotype of me as a Shell man was true. Was my personal identity characterized by the company for which I worked? Or was the company shaped and formed by the individuals who worked for it?

It seemed to me, on reflection, that *neither* was true. The institution was not a creation of its current members. It was a separate entity, a persona in its own right. It had its own character and history.

Joining the institution therefore meant a certain element of submission to a set of views and beliefs, which I might not have taken on as an individual—just as joining a church, a trade union, or a political party might lead one to support a set of practices and attitudes. But joining a corporation, any more than joining a church, a trade union, or a political party, did not mean surrendering my capacity for judgment or critical opinion. It meant that I would have to learn to exercise my judgment as a participant in a large, collective endeavor, however; my voice and the entity's voice might be distinct, but they would not be separate. For as long as I belonged to Shell, I would be associated with the Shell entity.

I had been half-insulted by the Brazilian press and politicians. It felt as though they were accusing me of things I had never done and accusing my father and my colleagues of the same things, by association. But now I realized that *I* wasn't being accused; the Shell *entity* was on trial, not me. At the same time, I was part of the Shell entity, and I racked my brains: Why haven't we got a clear answer? Managers at some of our competitors clearly felt the same way. This was the era, for instance, when Mobil Oil began to write and publish its argumentative newspaper ads, airing the company's point of view about oil politics, international trade, and environmental issues.

But Shell never created such ads. We talked about the possibility, and it became clear, in our conversations, that, although we had some answers as individuals, there was no answer available from the institution. We were part of an entity larger than ourselves. If we were going to come up with a fitting response, we would have to find a way to express the entity's needs and spirit. We would have to find a way to develop a healthy relationship between the entity's persona and its environment.

## The Persona of a Living Being

The concept of an entity's persona had already been part of my education for many years. I was introduced to it back in my college days in the 1950s, through the work of a significant German psychologist named William Stern. Though he is largely unknown outside continental Europe, Stern was one of the founders of developmental and learning psychology—best known, perhaps, for developing the intelligence quotient (IQ) formula. But it was his more philosophical writing that had the most impact on my understanding of the living company.

I was introduced to his ideas through an unusual path of study. Most business academics, particularly in the 1950s, began with the science of economics. This science, still recovering from its nineteenth-century struggle to gain scientific respectability, was focused on measurability, predictability, causality, and unambiguous answers. Academic credence, after all, could be acquired only by copying the approaches of hard sciences like physics. Thus, when economists talked about human behavior as part of their theories, they postulated a mythical creature, *Homo economicus:* a perfectly rational person who always operated from self-interest, with clearly defined reasons for every action and decision. Economic theory could thus encompass sophisticated formulas to describe complex, large-scale, aggregated activities, which then could be translated into "managerial science."

But the formulas said very little about the actual behavior of *Homo sapiens,* which is immeasurable, unpredictable, unfathomable, and deeply ambiguous. Even a 19-year-old student like me could tell, from my part-time job at a Shell refinery, that, whereas the management curriculum had no place for human beings, the workplace was full of them.

Indeed, five years of German occupation had made the workers of Holland into great masters of passive resistance to autocratic power pressures. The business results of Dutch companies could be clearly affected by recalcitrance, passive resistance, and the lack of active cooperation. Why, I wondered, why was so much time spent at university in understanding systems and figures and so little in understanding humans?

Seeking an answer, I opted to include general psychology in my doctoral studies. I was permitted to do this because, in addition to our major studies, such as economics, finance, and organizational structure, we were permitted two "lighter" electives. By some quirk which I never understood, a subject called general psychology figured in the list of electives. It was taught by a Dr. Van der Spek, the head of a nearby psychiatric institute. He seemed as surprised as anyone to find, in his charge, a student from the economics school, with no background in psychology and little time to follow courses (because my job at the Shell refinery kept me occupied with nearly full-time hours). The only way to combat ignorance was to give me a long list of books to read; thus, for the next year, I read my way through the history of psychological thought, through characterology, and on into modern schools like the existential psychology of Jean-Paul Sartre.

In this journey, my attention was caught, time and time again, by references to a school of thought called Personalismus, founded by William Stern. Stern became, with his wife Clara, one of the pioneers of child psychology. Together they operated a clinic and published a classic work on the language of children. He was one of the founders of a new university in Hamburg after World War I, and a forerunner to Jean Piaget. Then, in 1933, he and his wife were among the first victims of the Nazi persecution. Their clinic was closed; their books were banned and burned. The family took refuge in the United States. Stern died in Durham, North Carolina, in 1938, five years after he was forced into exile.

As far as I know, Stern never wrote in English. That explained why, despite his contributions, his name was little known. Outside Germany, few could read his papers. Within Germany, after 1933, his name, books, and reputation were wiped out. Only nearby Holland preserved his influence; there, with a sufficiently widespread knowledge of the German language, a group of academics seriously studied his ideas after World War II. His last book, *General Psychology on a Personalistic Basis,* was republished in 1950, in the German language, in The Hague.

I was drawn to Stern's thinking because of his systemic way of looking at human beings. Born in 1871, he had built a career in a discipline that, like economics, had to fight hard to earn the predicate "scientific." As with economics, academic respectability could be acquired only by copying the approaches of hard sciences like physics. Psychologists eschewed synthesis and generalization for analysis, specialization, and narrow definitions of their problems and studies. This led to the establishment of many specialized fields of study within psychology: Gestalt psychology, behaviorism, depth psychology, and more. All of them focused on *parts* of the human being: The subconscious, the reflexes of behavior, even the soul (as distinct from the body). Complicated phenomena, such as "seeing," were studied in the same ways that

physicists studied wave bands and electric currents. Fields of study were
kept narrow, so that experiments could achieve repeatable, predictable
results. And there were, indeed, important experimental results. But,
just as with economics, conventional psychology had very little to say
about the people at the Pernis refinery, where I worked after school,
and where so much understanding was needed.

Stern, by contrast, was trying to develop a *systemic theory,* a theory that would encompass the behavior of people in the refinery, the
Shell system around them, and the relationships that bound them together. As one fellow psychologist, R. B. MacLeod, put it,

> For [Stern,] psychology was simply a road leading towards an
> understanding of man, and ultimately towards an under-
> standing of the universe. . . . Stern preferred to regard his psy-
> chology as a special branch of a more general science of Per-
> sonalismus, a science which he hoped would one day unite
> within a single system the findings of all the sciences of man,
> the physiological, the psychological and the cultural-histori-
> cal.[2]

To Stern, each living being has an undifferentiated wholeness, with
its own character, which he called the *persona.* A living being cannot
be understood unless that persona becomes evident. The persona, in
fact, is the essence of the living being. It is part of the larger world, but
separated by its "membrane" from the larger world—made distinct as
a miniworld in itself, with its own values and experiences. The persona
represents body and soul together. And it has several key characteristics:

- **The persona is goal-oriented,** said Stern. It wants to live as long as
  possible and to realize the development of its potential from its talents and its aptitudes.
- **It is conscious of itself.** A persona can perceive itself as "I," although
  it is composed of parts and elements, which are personae in their own
  right. In its turn, it can be a part of a larger entity, as the soldier is
  part of a platoon, the platoon is part of a company, the company part

of an army, and the army part of a nation's armed forces. Stern condensed this concept into a Latin expression: "a *persona* is a Unitas Multiplex, a structure of structures."[3]

* **It is open to the outside world.** Elements from the outside—such as food, bacteria, dust, light, and sound vibrations—constantly enter the human system. But human individuals and their ideas also constantly enter higher-order personae such as a company or a corporation. At the same time, a persona is in constant relationship *with* the outside world, in the sense that every experience represents one more exchange in a lifelong dialogue with the forces of the world around it.
* **It is alive, but it has a finite lifespan.** One day it is born, and one day it will pass away.

In 1919, 60 years before the popularity of terms like *living systems, human potential,* and *holistic health,* Stern proposed looking at an entity's behavior, sociological environment, psychological history, and, by extension, economic life as components of one existence, all interrelated.

This resonated with me. I had hoped to find some understanding of the human being who, in my economics textbooks, had been abstracted to a lifeless marionette, the *Homo economicus.* Stern said, instead, that these lifeless marionettes were not people at all. The central argument of Stern's book *Person und Sache,* in fact, was the nature of the distinction between persons and things. "Things" are all the dead objects in the world, objects without a will or a life force. Things are impacted by events but do not decide to make things happen.

When the temperature goes up, the rock on the mountainside expands. When it freezes at night, the rock contracts. It may crack in the process, but in a very short time the rock is back in harmony with its cold environment. In the world of things, the world without a will, causality is measurable and repeatable. The same force, acting on a thing in the same way under the same conditions, once or a million times, will produce the same result. *Homo economicus* was thus a thing. It did not have a goal or a will; it existed only to react to other forces (such as supply and demand). The forces of the outside world might affect *Homo economicus* once, or a million times, under the same conditions; the result will always be the same.

By contrast, the members of *Homo sapiens*—the real people who work in real jobs or attend real schools—are unfathomable precisely because they are willful. They act toward their own purpose, which economists cannot predict.

A living entity, such as a human being, is not merely a passive object, buffeted by outside forces. As people, we make choices. Our behavior cannot be explained solely by cause-and-effect relationships. One cannot really say, "Such-and-such a thing happened to my next-door neighbor, and therefore, *of course*, he [or she] reacted in such-and-such a way." No one can guarantee how any of us would react in any given circumstances. Our individual behavior can be explained only by understanding the internal force of our goals and teleological drive, together with the forces coming from the outside environment. Even the same forces, striking twice under the same conditions, might not elicit the same reaction, for our internal goals might change. (We might, for example, have learned enough from the first strike to react differently the second time.)

Absorbing this insight from William Stern was very helpful to me during the years that followed. I cannot point to any specific decision that emerged from it, but it colored every decision I took and every move I made. I knew that I could not count on people to simply follow the rules, as if they were rational creatures. I knew that I could never predict their actions simply because they were alive. Although this unpredictability made the risks of business greater, it also meant I could tap potential rewards that would otherwise be closed to me. It meant that people would achieve, under encouraging conditions, great leaps of invention and activity that *Homo economicus* could never even dream of—if, that is, *Homo economicus* could dream at all.

But the events in Brazil of 1974, 20 years after my introduction to Stern, shook me up even further. As a result of my ruminations, I came to realize that Shell, as a whole, was also an unfathomable being. It, too, was alive. It, too, had potential rewards that could be tapped. Royal Dutch/Shell was not a thing. In the sense articulated by William Stern, Royal Dutch/Shell was alive.

## The Ladder

William Stern, as it happens, had anticipated my insight. In his work, he described a metaphorical ladder which might, if you drew it, look something like this:

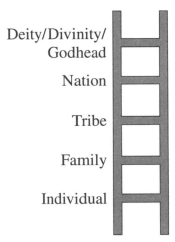

Deity/Divinity/
Godhead

Nation

Tribe

Family

Individual

Stern, of course, was writing this in 1919. Today, we would probably add some rungs below the level of individual, to include, perhaps, "body subsystems" and "cells." Everything in the ladder, larger or smaller than a human being, is a persona in its own right—or, as Stern called it, a "Unitas Multiplex."

Stern said that a living being always has a hierarchical structure. The ladder is the expression of that hierarchical structure. There are always smaller components within our personae, and we are always components of greater personae than ourselves. We are a *unitas multiplex,* he said; we are one, looked upon from the outside, and subdivided as seen from within.

In Stern's view, human individuals stand somewhere in the middle of the ladder of personae. Below them might be subsystems of the human body and even cellular identities. Actually, Stern was not specific about this; but more recent researchers, such as biologist/cybernetician Francisco Varela, have shown how subsystems such as the cell are actually organizations themselves, with collective entities and purposes.[4]

Above the human being on the ladder of personae are the collective organizations and institutions through which people join together. The family, the tribe, and the national government are all living systems in which people join together; so are the trade union, the sport club, and the nonprofit organization.

These living entities nest within each other, like Russian dolls. From the outside, one sees a large unit: Royal Dutch/Shell or the Catholic church (to give two examples). The newspapers speak of "Shell's activities in the North Sea" or the policies of *the* Catholic church. And this point of view is valid; there is a Royal Dutch/Shell persona, and there is a persona for the Catholic church. But that point of view is incomplete. For, seen from within, the order of the Jesuits is a living system on its own inside the Catholic church. Shell Brazil is a living system inside the Shell Group. Both the Jesuits and Shell Brazil are driven by self-preservation and self-development, as much as the higher order systems of which they are a subordinated part.

Further down the ladder within each of these entities, one sees a variety of individual people, each with individual goals, striving toward survival and self-development. The individual people are often symbiotic, but equally often they end up clashing with each other. Each has different characteristics and potential.

A company like Royal Dutch/Shell, in short, has its own ladder of personae, looking something like this:

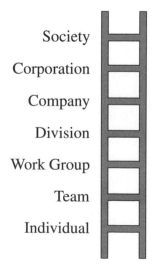

Society

Corporation

Company

Division

Work Group

Team

Individual

Each unit of a company, at its own level, is a living system. Each is distinct, visible, and self-determined. At the same time, each unit is embedded in the larger whole.

Consider how these units match William Stern's criteria for a living persona.

- Each of these units is goal oriented. Each is driven toward self-preservation and self-development. No matter what individual managers might feel, each business unit continues to act to preserve itself and expand its scope of activity.

    As with an individual person, the behavior of a corporation (or of its units) cannot be explained solely through external cause and effect. For example, one cannot say that Japanese competition or lowered profits *caused* General Motors to react by changing its product line. GM's behavior, in the face of competition or lowered profits, can be explained only by understanding the various living systems within GM. Perhaps Cadillac changed its product line one way, because of its own goal to sell more expensive cars, while Chevrolet responded in a thoroughly different way, because of a goal of better-quality cars. Or, in its response, General Motors might merely have been part of a larger response by the American automobile industry. Whatever happened, the behavior of General Motors is unpredictable; no one can guarantee that events would play out the same way a second time.

- Each unit of the company is conscious of itself. Everyone associated with any of these units is aware of its boundaries, of who is included and excluded. The fate of Shell Brazil, for example, is clearly linked to the fate of its customers, its suppliers, its retail station franchise holders. But no one assumes that Petrobras, which is Shell's major supplier in that country, is a part of Shell Brazil.

- Each unit is open to the outside world. People and ideas continually enter and leave a company, in the same way that a human being exchanges information and material through his or her digestive system, pores, eyes, and ears. Just about every corporate experience, from mundane transactions to intricate scenario exercises, represents one more exchange in a constant, lifelong dialogue with the forces of the world around the organization.

- Each unit of a company, while alive, has a finite lifespan. One day, each of the operating companies within Royal Dutch/Shell will pass away. Some will die before Royal Dutch/Shell dies. Some may live on past that time, as components that become part of other corporations. Each organizational unit has a potential lifespan, which it may or may not reach.

You might argue that, whereas you are an individual being, a corporation is simply a construct, composed of creatures. It may contain many personae, but it is not alive in the same way, for example, that a human being is alive. But within your body, there are cells, viruses, bacteria, intruders, and parasites, often acting without your conscious control, and sometimes (for example, when you get the flu) varying from your purpose. A company contains managers, employees, shareholders, subsidiary companies, buildings, technologies, and financial assets. Both of these personae, you and the company, thrive best when most of the small entities are reasonably well dedicated to the survival and potential of the whole.

For most businesspeople, the implications of this ladder are a bit harsh. Managers would prefer the world of business to be like the world of things: always in harmony with its environment, passive without a will of its own, just waiting for the manager to give it a push, which would then produce a predictable and measurable result. Instead, as a living entity, a company is always insecure, never stable, always subject to shifting relationships between the company and the outside world.

And, with that understanding, in 1974 I began to see a way out of my dilemma at Shell Brazil—to define the way that Shell Brazil could stand for itself while remaining open to its outside environment.


## Introception


There is another point about living entities: they are the only entities that can learn. Cybernetician/biologist Francisco Varela expresses the idea this way: "Every living being that moves, has a brain." A brain allows learning. Where there is movement, there is learning.

In my talks, I put forth the hypothesis that "companies can learn."

I encounter little skepticism. I rarely add the rest of the sentence: "Companies can learn *because* they are living beings." If they were mere "bundles of assets," they would be dead objects, and learning would be impossible for them.

I admit that it comes to me relatively easily to think of companies, or indeed every institution (trade unions, clubs, churches, government organizations) as "persons" or "living systems." The same is true for legislation in nearly every Western country: corporations tend to come under the legal definition of "persons." And everyday language grants corporations the same courtesy: we speak of "General Motors deciding," or "Unilever marketing a product." The way we speak of a corporation is much closer to our language about human individuals than to the way we would speak about a lump of ore or a sack of grain.

But why should it be important that corporations can learn? In part, it is important because of a faculty called "introception." William Stern described this capability, common to all learning beings: the ability to be aware of one's own stance and position vis-à-vis the rest of the world.

Stern suggested that introception was one of three types of interactions between an entity and the world around it. The first level was simply a *biological* relationship to the threat, stimuli, raw materials, and accommodation of the environment. Is it hot? Is there food? Does the environment excite us? Does it scare us? Animals live mostly at this biological level.

The second level of interaction involves *direct experiences* and encounters with the world when we feel harmony with it. These experiences are stored in the memory of the persona and recalled selectively, to accentuate the positive. For as long as possible, we seek to live in peace with our environment. We may feel tensions with it, as mismatches occur, but we will try to put them aside.

However, sometimes the tension exceeds a threshold beyond which we cannot tolerate it any longer, and we reach a crisis. Now we enter a third level: the level of *values and beliefs*. We don't need a crisis to reach this level; we can also get there through sustained reflection. But once here, all our principles and attitudes are open to question in light of the values and attitudes of our environment. Do we agree, for example, with the prevailing attitudes about ethics and virtue—attitudes that may be laid down by authority figures, such as our parents or our bosses? If we disagree, how strongly do we rebel against them? How do we reconcile our differences from the prevailing sensibility of the larger system? To Stern, questions like these thrust people (and companies) into a process of building greater awareness, a process which he called "introception."

Stern wrote that introception was a key function of the persona of complex entities. They must find their place in the world; they must develop a sense of the relationship between their own persona's ethical priorities and the values in the surrounding world. For example, a living company is always engaged in questioning its own value system in relation to the ethics of the world in which it lives. This process is directly linked to the company's persona, which may in fact date back to before the current legal incarnation.

A consultant named Michael McMaster, for instance, recently described how he visited a construction company in the northeast of England, a company based at an old shipyard. Already it was possible to see how the company's current work—manufacturing parts of North Sea oil drilling platforms—would disappear over time, as construction of new North Sea platforms stopped. How would the company cope? The managers weren't sure until, after some prodding, they began looking back at their own history. There had always been an economic activity based in that estuary, drawing its labor pool and membership from the local community. They had built Viking ships there once; then they had built windjammers, and then steam engines. Now they were building ocean platforms. What would come next? They could not be sure, but it would involve finding a harmony between the regional physical environment (the proximity to the sea) and the human capability that had existed there for centuries. This land, this community, was deeply entwined with the company's persona, and they could change that persona only with great, wrenching effort and risk.

The historian Simon Schama describes a different sort of dance between corporate values and the ethics of its environment in seventeenth-century Holland, when a society in transition tried to make space for new forms of commercial enterprise.

> [The strong Calvinist] sense of the reprehensible nature of
> money-making persisted, even while the Dutch amassed their

individual and collective fortunes. The odd consequence of this disparity between principle and practice was to foster expenditure . . . (notably), acts of conspicuous expenditure on both pious objects . . . ( and on) propitiatory gestures of philanthropy.[5]

Sensitive to the world, the new commercial enterprises adapted—not just by being more philanthropical than would have come naturally, but also by fomenting institutional change:

The safest place of all in Amsterdam was its Wisselbank, founded in 1609. . . . Its overriding concern was not to generate funds for enterprise, but, on the contrary, to control the conditions under which they could be exchanged. . . . Its very existence testified to a determination to neutralize the worst evils associated with the unconfined world of money: usury, default, counterfeit and other kinds of fraud. Its working motto was "probity, not profit."[6]

In the relationship between the persona of the corporation and the persona of the local government, neither may be affected immediately. One may overpower the other in the end. But both sides will inevitably be affected by the other's value systems, because, as we will see, both are influenced by the same critical factor: the values of the people who belong to them both.

## When the Persona and the World Don't Match

Companies like Shell often find themselves in the sort of dilemma that engulfed me in Brazil in 1974. There is a mismatch between the company's sense of "rightness" and fair play, and the ethics of the society around it. Such dilemmas can be gravely serious; they can call into question the fundamental values of a manager's life.

At Royal Dutch/Shell, for example, the Statement of Business Principles says that it is *verboten* to pay bribes or grant favors to local politicians. But, in many countries, bribing local ministers is an accepted way of doing business. In other countries, such as the Brazil I knew in 1974, the prevailing ethics of the host country seems irreversibly bent on criticizing a company, just for existing and doing business within its borders. And, in still other countries, such as South Africa of the late 1970s and early 1980s, a politically reprehensible regime is in place, and outsiders call upon corporations to leave the country entirely.

In these difficult situations, should the company refrain from operating in that country? Should the company refrain from hiring local people? Finally, what responsibility does a company have to an environment where its values and principles, its persona, seems horribly out of place?

As I began to think about these questions in terms of William Stern's theory, it became apparent that the most intuitively appealing solution—holding fast to one's own moral principles and leaving the country—would often do the most damage in the long run.

During the late 1970s, I was the coordinator in charge of a region that included Africa. At that time, the senior management of Royal Dutch/Shell was under great pressure from activists in the United States, Sweden, and Holländ to shut down its South African subsidiary. Shell's presence in South Africa, and the oil it supplied, were seen to give legitimacy and power to the apartheid system. For years, the senior managers at Royal Dutch/Shell agonized about this. We were basically decent people, and we knew as well as our critics about apartheid's devastating effects; we saw them directly, and we didn't like it. My colleagues and I thought seriously about adding our voices to the protests and supporting the removal of Shell from South Africa.

Yet, in the end, we chose to remain. Personally, I had two reasons. First, protesting was not a role we understood at Shell. We were very good at producing and distributing oil and gas. We were not sure we knew how to effectively manage a withdrawal of this scale and significance. The assets, such as refineries and depots, could not be removed. The people to operate them were mostly South African. Withdrawal risked being an empty gesture of high morals, but low practical value.

The second reason had to do with introception. Stern's theory suggested that, if you want to truly change society, you could only accomplish it from the inside out—from the clash of different value systems in a single environment. Even while I agreed that the apartheid system had to change, I was convinced that only working from the inside, as part of the South African community, could we change it. Kicking at them from the outside would not work. The government that maintained apartheid would not call upon its introception to deal with us, if we moved outside the country. We would simply become one more enemy to be ignored. Within the country, we were one of the forces affecting South Africa's sense of its own identity.

In making this decision, I drew upon two previous experiences in African nations. When I took over as regional coordinator of Africa in 1978, we had just shut down Shell Angola. There had been a revolution there, fueled by Marxist ideology and East German advisers. My predecessor had let himself be convinced that the new environment was dangerous for Shell people. Unwilling to risk the lives of any Shell employees, he shut down Shell Angola and walked out of the country.

Shortly afterward, our offices were visited by an Angolan government delegation, led by one of the victorious generals of the revolution, who had now become minister of energy. He still called himself by his *nom de guerre:* General Monty. We made no headway during the morning. He had brought a delegation, we had a group of managers, and he spoke very little English. But at lunch, I made sure we were sitting across from each other. After my time in Brazil, I spoke Portuguese— one of the languages common in Angola. Probably none of the other Shell people spoke it. So I began talking to him in Portuguese over lunch, and his eyes lit up. Finally he could say what was on his mind.

"You're a bloody coward," he said. "You walked out of the country."

"Sure," I said. "It was dangerous for our people. When you marched up to Luanda [the capital] shooting, we had to leave."

"Maybe," he said. "But you're Shell. You're big, visible, and basically nonpolitical. When you walked out, you gave the start signal for a flight out of Angola."

It was true; in the 1970s, there had been a major refugee flight back to Lisbon from Angola. Once Shell left, everyone with a Portuguese passport wanted to leave as well. This meant that, almost overnight, the middle class in Angola disappeared. The shopkeepers, mechanics, engineers, station owners, and the people who ran the telephone company all considered themselves Portuguese, even though they often had a great deal of African blood.

"When you whistled," the minister continued, "they fled. And you did tremendous damage to our country. Admittedly, Mobil took over, but Shell's example was influential. When Shell whistled, they fled."

The infrastructure delivering aviation fuel to the airfields and gasoline to the service stations began to break down as a result, he said. Because they were still fighting the war, nearly all of the available supply that survived Shell's exit was requisitioned by the military. Now that the war was over, the country had enormous difficulty maintaining and developing the infrastructure to function as a nation-state.

"That's why you're a bloody coward," he repeated.

That conversation stayed with me a long time. He had given me something to think about, something on which I ruminated for years.

Soon thereafter, another African revolution took place—in Ethiopia. The emperor was thrown out, and a group of Soviet-supported Marxists took charge. They instituted a series of totalitarian initiatives, including the "Red Neighborhood" committees. Anyone with a Western connection (such as working for a multinational company) was susceptible to being taken from bed in the early morning, tortured during the day, and shot at dusk.

It could have been very easy to shut down Shell Ethiopia. It was a relatively small company. But the top man, a young man of Scottish descent, deeply impressed me. He had made up his mind that he wanted to stay in the country. At 6:30 each morning he stood by the door to the Shell office and counted the employees. If one was missing, by 9:00 A.M. he had sent out emissaries to find him or her. They were often in the hands of a Red Neighborhood committee. By lunchtime, he was at the Ministry of War office. "There is one of my people in the hands of that committee," he would say. "If he isn't back by five this afternoon, I will stop supplying the army with oil."

We lost only one employee in the revolution. When it ended, Shell was the only Western multinational company still working in Ethiopia. All the others had packed their bags and left. Except for Shell, the entire infrastructure and production capacity of the country was unmanned. Two years later, the revolutionary communist regime allowed us to start paying dividends to our shareholders. We still run that company, primarily with Ethiopians as managers. It is one of their very few opportunities to learn managerial skills without leaving the country.

Those two experiences taught me that we could only define our responsibility situationally—vis-à-vis the larger communities in which we worked. In thinking about South Africa, I had come to the conclusion that it was an undeniably unpleasant regime. But there were many unpleasant regimes in the territory for which I was responsible, which stretched from Morocco to Burma. The most unpleasant regimes were often almost invisible to outside activist groups. We deeply disliked them, but we did not step out of them. Our responsibility was to produce material wealth, and we contributed, in the process, to the introception of these repressive regimes.

Indeed, over the years Shell has seen many countries change their value systems. South Africa moved into apartheid in the 1950s; it moved out of apartheid 30 years later. Every time such a change occurs, the company, like the other inhabitants of the country, runs the risk that the value system of this part of its world will begin to diverge from its own. The company has the same choice that individuals have: to either adapt or walk away. Walking away, boycotting, or sanctions would not move that country closer to the company's value system.

William Stern articulated the complexity of this relationship, based in the introception of corporation and state.

> The Persona has an influence on the world around it as an example, a "role model," but it can never equalize the world's values with its own. On the other hand, neither can the world completely impose its values on an individual country. Moreover, the mutual influence is weak in the present. *The most important effect of the radiation of persona on society and the infection of the persona by society will take place in the future.* The examples given by ideas and work need time to be absorbed.[7]

Is it always an argument for remaining, no matter how terrible the regime? I think, with one exception, that the answer is yes. And the exception is: You only remain if you are given a choice. Every regime that starts killing, nationalizing, or expelling you does not offer that choice, and so you should leave. Examples in the Shell history include Russia after 1917 and China after 1946, when Shell withdrew from those nations. Other examples include the Jews who left Germany during the 1930s.

I have come to believe that a multinational company, working in more than 100 of the world's countries, can only choose to be itself and to remain truthful to its persona. If given a choice, it should stay; but this means being neutral to the political values embraced in many of the host countries. If we chose to work in only those value systems where we felt comfortable, in the end we would operate in only about 15 percent of the world's countries. And we would give up, in the process, our persona's opportunity to contribute to the world.

## Who Belongs?

During my Shell time, I was continuously aware of the level of "membership" in everyone I met. I could encounter a salesman in East Africa or a depot foreman in North Pakistan and know of him—as he would know of me—that he was one of us, a Shell person whom I could trust. On the other hand, I could meet a nonexecutive board member, not recognize him as a Shell person, and know automatically that he did not think of himself as one of us either. This was not necessarily a bad thing. In some cases, a nonexecutive director should *not* belong. Similarly, external auditors who spent most of their working life auditing the Shell account, learning more about the company than just about anyone internally, were *still* not "one of us."

However large or small the membership, the need for cohesion between the members exists in all organizations, not just companies. In a church, the harmony between the value system of the members and that of the institution must be particularly strong. A confession of faith is thus required of all new members. A soldier in a country's army cannot object, in principle, to the values of that army; otherwise, the recruit is forced into civil service instead of military service. And at the Royal Dutch/Shell Group, a new member must subscribe to the company's Statement of Business Principles. Violation of these principles is viewed as a serious offense, usually followed by expulsion.

The ham-fisted mergers and downsizings of recent years tend to tear companies apart precisely because they confound this need for cohesion. These types of changes put enormous pressure on the persona at the heart of the company's identity. They strain the linkages between the values of the company and the values of its members. Managers are forced to ask themselves, "Am I still a member of this firm? Is my membership secure?"

If this argument is persuasive, you may be ready to accept the idea that a company is primarily a living being. But a question probably remains: What does this mean for management? Is managing a living system different from managing a company in the traditional way, as a collection of assets? Can a living company be managed in the same way as an economic company? Yes, a company may be alive. It may have a persona. But so what?

# 6

# Managing for Profit or for Longevity

*Is There a Choice?*

DURING THE LAST FEW YEARS, THE PROBLEMS WITH WHOLESALE staff reductions have become well known in business. Managers are familiar with the costs of overloading the staff who remain, of losing loyalty, and of having to hire back new staff with less commitment and capability, when the business expands again. We understand all of these costs, yet we continue to cut staff routinely whenever return on investment (ROI) must be improved.

The reason is that we do not place the cutbacks in the context of the real nature of our companies. There are, in fact, two different types of commercial companies in existence today, distinguished by their primary reason for being in business. The first type of company is run for a purely "economic" purpose: to produce maximum results with minimum resources. This sort of "economic company" is managed primarily for profit. People are regarded as "assets"—extensions of the capital assets of the firm. As with capital assets, investment in human assets is held to a minimum in an economic company, to produce the greatest possible return in the shortest amount of time.

The economic company is not a work community, except incidentally. It is a corporate machine. Its sole purpose is the production of wealth for a small inner group of managers and investors. It feels no responsibility to the membership as a whole. It provides no community for its employees and managers, except as a by-product of its chief purpose: return on investment in capital and human assets.

This economic company represents a viable choice. Many people in the business world may not want to create a work community. It is perfectly legitimate for anybody to want to have a corporate machine with the sole purpose of earning a living for that person or for his or her family. Moreover, it is also philosophically viable. Assets *are* important, and so is the return on investment. Without these financial concepts, civilization would never have developed its current ability to produce wealth. But making this choice has consequences.

Here, as everywhere, there is no free lunch. People who run economic companies have far fewer options in their managerial practices. Only a small group of people qualify to be "one of us" in the inner circle. All other people recruited to contribute to the corporate efforts will become attachments to somebody else's money machine. They will be outsiders, recruited for their skills. They will not be members. They trade their time and expertise for money, and they feel little loyalty to the company as an entity. They may even feel little trust for the people in the company, and certainly little desire to give their all on the firm's behalf. This means that hierarchical controls must be strengthened. Otherwise, the economic machine will not work effectively. Strong hierarchical controls mean that conditions are reduced for the effective mobilization of the brain capacity of all the people in the firm.

If this economic business should grow somewhat, then new members will have to be admitted to the inner core of the company. These new members will, inevitably, be chosen by the founders. They may include family members or close friends. The "people who belong" will continue to consist of as small a group as possible. Potential recruits will understand that, although they may be recruited, they are not there to stay. They will work with their eventual exit in mind.

A critical point will inevitably arrive, one day, when the succession of the inner community will have to be addressed. The founder, or his or her successor, will leave. This shows up the second inherent weakness of economic companies. Not only is it more difficult for them to be a learning organization, but they also face considerable obstacles in the transition from one management generation to the next.

To me, an economic company is like a puddle of rainwater—a collection of raindrops, gathered together in a cavity or hollow. These drops *are* the puddle. They remain in their position, at the bottom of the cavity. When it rains, more drops may be added to the puddle; its field of influence may broaden, soaking the ground around it. But those central, original drops remain in their position at the middle.

Paradoxically, this stability may lead to vulnerability. Puddles of rainwater cannot survive much heat. When the sun shines and the temperature heats up, the puddle starts evaporating. Even the drops at the very center, in the middle of a heat wave, are in danger of going up in vapor. In fact, most puddles have very short lifespans.

That is the *economic company*.

The second type of company, by contrast, is organized around the purpose of perpetuating itself as an ongoing community. This type of company has the longevity of a river. Unlike a puddle, a river is a permanent feature of its landscape. Come rain, the river may swell. Come shine, the river may shrink. But it takes a long and severe drought for the river to disappear.

Yet from the point of view of the drops of water, the river is horribly turbulent. No drop of water remains at the center for very long. From one moment to the next, the water in one part of the river or another will have changed. It will no longer be the same. Finally, the drops of water run out to the sea. The river lasts many times longer than the lifetime of the individual drops of water which comprise it.

Instead of stagnating like a puddle, long-lasting companies seem to emulate the flow of a river. No one drop of water dominates the company for long; indeed, new water drops continually succeed the old drops and then in their turn are carried out to sea. The drops of water are not destroyed; they are carried forward. The river is a self-perpetuating community, with component water drops that enter and leave, with its own built-in guarantees for the continuity and motion of water within its banks. A company, by initiating rules for continuity and motion of its *people,* can emulate the longevity and power of the river.

In such a "river company," return on investment remains important. But managers regard the optimization of capital as a complement to the optimization of people. The company itself is *primarily* a community. Its purposes are longevity and the development of its own potential. Profitability is a means to that end. And to produce both profitability and longevity, care must be taken with the various processes for building a community: defining membership, establishing common values, recruiting people, developing their capabilities, assessing their potential, living up to a human contract, managing relationships with outsiders and contractors, and establishing policies for exiting the company gracefully.

To create a company that flows like a river, we must consider the design of the channels that contain the flow.

## The Boundaries of Identity

A river company is open to the outside world: There is tolerance for a high entry of new individuals and ideas. It is, in fact, *expected* that new concepts and knowledge will flow through the company's "stream of activity" on an everyday basis.

At the same time, however, the river company maintains its cohesive identity. Members know "who is us," and they are aware that they hold values in common. In a very real sense, they belong to each other. In Chapter 5, "Only Living Beings Learn," I described "introception" as the awareness of one's own values and how those mesh with the values of the outside world. But another sort of introception exists within most companies. The values of the company coexist with the values of individuals *within* the corporation—and every member is aware of this coexistence.

A company has a collective sense of the answer to the definitive question about corporate identity: Who belongs? Who is considered part of "us"? Conversely, who does *not* belong, and thus is part of the surrounding world?

There is no ambiguity about who belongs and who does not. At the level of introception, the company's members know who is prepared to live with the company's set of values. Whoever cannot live with those values, cannot or should not be a member. Whoever is not a member does not need to share the values. However, they can share the values of some other institution, like a trade union, and still be an employee-nonmember of this company. Of course, these nonmembers are likely to act as nonmembers, putting the needs of some other entity before the needs of the company. Members must share the set of institutional values that rest at the core of the company's persona.

At Shell, we saw this in our research on corporate longevity, the study described in the Prologue. Even in companies that were widely diversified or decentralized, the employees and management often seemed to have a rather good understanding of "what this company stands for," or "what this company is about." And they happily identified themselves with these principles.

In many cases, this value system had been brought in by the founder. Sometimes it was even formalized in a sort of constitution. As the report noted:

> One company saw itself as a fleet of ships, each ship independent, yet the whole fleet stronger than the sum of its parts. This sense of belonging to an organization and being able to identify with its achievements can easily be dismissed as a soft or abstract feature of change. But case histories showed that strong employee links were essential for survival and change. Successful companies appear to maintain a cohesion at all levels.[1]

Cohesion is the force with which the molecules of a body cleave together. In a company, cohesion represents the pulling together (and *keeping* together) of the employees. To have cohesion, employees must know "who belongs" and "who is not one of us."

In a living company, cohesion and diversity exist together. The company is clearly a unit, with a single identity; but the people and substructures within that unit show a rich variety. They are composed differently from each other; they have different characteristics and different potential. But they are all part of a cohesive whole. Shell Brazil, for example, has quite different characteristics from Deutsche Shell's. As substructures, however, they work together organically in the worldwide Shell Group. In the same way, Deutsche Shell, subdivided in its turn, will expect its own substructures—its divisions, refineries, and marketing districts—to work organically for the company as a whole.

This insight helps us maintain some optimism about widely divergent systems like a multinational company (or the Catholic church or a cooperative of Raiffeisen banks). These systems can hold together.

The substructures—the individual operating companies, monasteries, and churches, or cooperating savings banks—*do not need to be made uniform for the whole to keep together*. On the contrary, there is value in diversity. Nor do they need to be controlled by hierarchical submission. Cohesion takes place on a more ephemeral, yet completely tangible, level.

Cohesion with variety may mean that the company has members with whom we do not necessarily feel a deep emotional sympathy. Cohesion can mean being stuck with people we dislike. This, I believe, is a blessing in disguise. One day, early in my career, my boss (the finance controller of a Shell operating company) called me in to give me an exciting new assignment: "We are going to start a new department—Methods & Procedures—and you are to be its boss."

My department would undertake a thorough redesign—what would now be called a "reengineering"—of the old accounting and administrative processes. We would build a new department out of nothing! I listened happily as the controller read out the names of people who would be transferred to this new department. But then he came, at the end of the list, to Mr. Z.

I jumped from my chair. "Oh no, not Mr. Z!" Two years earlier, I had worked directly under Mr. Z in another section of the accounts department. We had argued heatedly. I did not like him as a person; I thought he was a blustery braggart. "All air, no substance," I judged, with the absolute certainty of a 23-year-old.

"Young man," said the controller (who had always been a mentor to me), "you will have to learn one or two things, and this is a good time in your life to do it. First, if you want to be a leader, you must realize that a manager is not God. A manager does not create people—certainly not in his own image. As a manager you take people as they come, the way God created them, and you learn to work with them."

He let that message sink in before he continued: "Second, in working with people, you should learn that it is inefficient to try to make up for their 'imperfections' (as you consider them) by working harder or longer hours yourself. By doing so, you may increase your output by 25 percent or 30 percent over a limited period. You might gain one-third of a man-year. However, if you create the conditions under which 10 people will each produce 10 percent more, you will have gained one full man-year."

I did not contest the logic of his argument.

"So, Mr. Z is going to work with you," he concluded. "If, at any time, I hear of a disagreement between the two of you, I will not bother to find out the cause. It will be your fault! As a manager you have to learn to work with people as you find them. Your role is to create the conditions in which they will voluntarily give their best."

Mr. Z and I worked together for two years. I forced myself to listen to him, even when I disagreed. Only once I exploded. I felt a red curtain of anger rising in me, and I asked Mr. Z, "Please, go and close the door of my office on the outside." He did so. I turned and walked to the window, picked up a steel ruler from a table, and broke it between my hands.

Mr. Z, for his part, went straight from my office to visit the controller. I only found this out at the end of the year, however, when the whole episode was included in my performance report—no doubt reducing my performance bonus.

Mr. Z and I continued to work together for more than two years. Indeed, I had to learn that part of my job involved creating conditions in which even he was moved to give his best. Mr. Z and I, after all, were members of a common entity, and it was my duty *to that entity* to find his strong points and help bring the maximum out of them. Mr. Z and I needed more than mere tolerance of each other. We would have to become aligned, with a sense of common values and purpose. But that mutual sensibility could not exist unless we knew, down to our bones, that we were members of the same common whole and therefore could trust each other even if we did not like each other.

## Common Values

Is there no alternative to either killing the diversity of a company or beating the organization into hierarchical submission? In other words, what keeps the members of a river company in tune with each other?

They subscribe to a set of common values. They believe that the goals of the company will help them to achieve their own individual goals. Or, as William Stern put it:

It is important that the individual goals of the substructures are harmonious with and best served by the goals of the higher level system. In crude terms, this means that the overarching structure should make it clear and prove to its components down to the individual human beings, that their survival and their self actualization are best served by working together towards the survival and the development of the whole.[2]

This basic "egoistic" principle is often misunderstood in business governance. It means that anyone running a large, complex institution—such as a group of subsidiary companies, a set of joint ventures, or a company composed of business units—cannot simply dominate individual self-interest through the exercise of power. As Stern might put it, each entity within a company, from the subsidiaries to the business units to the departments to the individuals, is a persona in its own right. Each of these personae exists in constant exchange and dialogue with the world around it. This means that each is continually testing its own values, through introception, against those of the larger group. Governance is a matter of assuring that the goals of the subsidiary companies and of each employee are harmonious with the goals of the larger whole—and vice versa.

A key governance issue, for example, involves the perennial problem of the salaries paid to top managers. Press accounts often excoriate CEOs and senior managers for making too many times the salary of people at the lower ends of the hierarchy. This *is* a problem, but not for outsiders. It is a critical question for a company's introception about its own values.

Any executive's remuneration is exaggerated if it is experienced by the rest of the work community as exaggerated. One work community might be quite prepared to pay its top people fairly high amounts; that would be in harmony with the company's internal realities. Another work community would find high salaries for senior managers unpalatable. The standard for any pay scale is an internal standard. You may be my boss today, but I'm the next generation. I know I'll be the boss tomorrow, or one of my peers will.

The goals, in short, of each member must be harmonized with the goals of the whole community. The whole and the parts must understand that the interests of each are best served by staying together.

Many people seem to want this form of cohesion. It's what they're describing when they say, for example, "I spend eight hours or more every day at work. It's a dominant part of my life. And I want it to fit with the rest of my life!"

Our corporate survivor study at Shell revealed a very suggestive link between long-lived companies and a strong sense of values. In some companies, these values hailed back to the founder of the company. This person might even have codified a kind of mission statement, describing a vision of what he wanted the company to be. This would be a statement of what the company is about: A definition of *self.*

This should not be confused with the typical "corporate vision and mission statements" prominent in companies today. Today's mission statements are written in the future tense. They talk about "what the company will be." This makes them negative, in the sense that they tell the members what their company is *not* at this moment, but what it would like to be at some moment in the future. They are explicit; they define the company as a "computer firm," or an "oil producer" (admittedly the best in the world!). Thus they overlook a critical question: What will bind together the members of this work community, when the world moves away from computers or from oil?

Founders and managers of long-lived companies, a hundred years or more in the past, did not link their values to a particular product, service, or line of work. They knew, or sensed, that the life mission of a work community was *not* to produce a particular product or service, but to *survive:* to perpetuate itself as a work community. Their statements contained values and ethical rules akin to a modern "statement of business principles" or to the basic tenets of a religion. Members, future and present, of that company would have to make these values and rules their own, or else they would not deserve their place in that company. More likely than not, in deeply troubled times when nobody knew the answer to totally new problems, the sharing of a set of common values helped companies make choices to which all the individual employees could subscribe. They were sailing blindly into an uncertain future, but they could have confidence and belief in each other.

Consider, for example, the story of the Japanese company Mitsui, a drapery shop that became a moneylender and then a mining and manufacturing enterprise. The founder, Takatoshi Mitsui, left behind a large set of rules and guidelines when he died in 1694. These included some *organizational principles:*

> Those in authority should be kind to subordinates, who in return should respect those in authority.

> The essential role of managers is to guard the business of the House. They should give appropriate advice if their masters' conduct is not good and correct blunders that may be made.

There were rules on *personnel management:*

> Considerable amounts of silver shall be set aside as a reserve fund for the benefit of elderly employees of the House who have lost their property and also for the relief of those suffering from fire and other calamities.

> In order to select for managers, keep an eye on the young men and train promising candidates for that position.

Other rules describe the *ethics* of conducting business:

> Farsightedness is essential to the career of a merchant. In pursuing small interests close at hand, one may lose huge profits in the long run.

> All kinds of speculation and new and unfamiliar business ventures shall be strictly forbidden.

> Persons in public office are not, as a rule, prosperous. This is because they concentrate on discharging their public duties and neglect their own family affairs. Do not forget you are a merchant. You must regard dealing with the government always as a sideline of your business.

These values and rules helped many generations of Mitsui people to see who they were and what they stood for. Learning starts with self-knowledge. A distinctive definition of self improves cohesion.

The results in the case of Mitsui were impressive. The corporation became the Japanese government's official moneychanger in the eighteenth century. Yet, in the nineteenth century, it was adaptable enough to switch political allegiance and thus survive the Meiji Restoration. In the twentieth century, Mitsui covered almost every type of commercial, industrial, and financial activity through more than 100 subsidiaries. Then came the severest test of its cohesion and adaptability.

In 1945 President Harry S Truman issued a directive: The industrial/banking combines, such as Mitsui, that dominated the Japanese economy would be dissolved. The Shell report describes the consequences.

> Holding companies of the Zaibatsu combines were liquidated and the wealth of the Zaibatsu families was drastically reduced by a heavy capital levy. The two greatest trading houses, Mitsui Bussan and Mitsubishi Sjohi were forced to liquidate in 1947. To prevent them starting up again, the dissolution order prohibited any company from employing more than two former officers or one hundred employees. As a result, Mitsui Bussan dissolved into 170 separate companies. In addition, the use of such trade names as Mitsui and Mitsubishi was forbidden.

One might expect this is enough to annihilate any corporate entity. Mitsui's money was taken away, its managerial capacity dissolved, its name rubbed out, and its central nervous system (the management structure and trading facilities) liquidated. What could possibly still be alive to grow back into a living system?

The Shell report recounts the sequel.

> A movement towards reunion of the Zaibatsu groups started after the termination of the occupation (1952). Although the top holding company was still missing, leaders of the former Zaibatsu companies organized regular meetings for the pur-

pose of information exchange, and the bank, to which several companies looked for lines of credit, began to perform some of the central functions. The companies resumed old names with Mitsui (in it) and the separated dissolved trading companies merged to form Mitsui-Busan (1959).

These days, Mitsui is thought to be the name of a group composed of about 30 companies. Some of these put Mitsui with their own names. The relationship among these companies is informal but it can sometimes be substantial. (For example, Mitsui Petro Chemical was founded by eight companies of the Mitsui group in 1965.) Although the Mitsui Zaibatsu has been dead since the dissolution, the identity of "Mitsui" seemed to be kept alive within the companies of the group.

To what extent did the sharing of a set of common values make this remarkable resurrection possible? It could not have been negligible. Only a sense of common identity—a feeling of belonging to a social system with a strong definition of self—could have surmounted the destruction of the original unit into its separate cells and genes. This collective sense of self was even stronger than the ambitions and greed of the managers who had been placed in charge of the individual companies after the dissolution. They could have "gone it alone," and in the short run, they would have been successful. But they were too infused with Mitsui's values to leave the name and the entity behind.

You might be inclined to dismiss this example because Mitsui is Japanese, and thus culturally inclined toward collectivism. But the Deutsche Bank in Germany was similarly fragmented by occupying forces, and it returned full strength, under its original name. At the same time, other companies in the Axis nations did not survive the dissolution of the postwar period. The industrial empire of I. G. Farben, for example, was broken up into smaller chemical companies, including BASF and Hoechst, which never came together again. In many instances they engaged in strong competition with each other.

## Joining the Flow: Recruitment Policies

River companies are very selective in the people they admit to their membership. But they cannot be closed. Like the water in a river, the membership of the community is constantly changing. Sometimes members are forced out, when their value system is apparently not harmonious with the company's values. Sometimes a small group of members redefines "who is us" and "who is not." Attention must always be given to ensuring a regular stream of new talent to refresh the company.

Cohesive recruitment is not so much a matter of policy; it is a form of reasoning. It starts by defining the desirable size and shape of the human community. You may assume, for example, that the total size of the company's membership will stay more or less constant during the foreseeable future. How many people must then be fed into the stream to compensate for all the people lost during the next 25 years to retirement, resignations, and ill health?

Then repeat this exercise under a number of different assumptions. Assume 10 percent growth, for example. Assume that one particular corporate unit will grow disproportionately. As you consider each of these scenarios for potential growth, you will discover that a figure begins to crystallize: a target for annual and regular recruitment. This is a *target* figure, because a company can never be sure that in each individual year it will find (or can afford) the exact number of people of the required qualifications—the necessary academic or technical backgrounds, the required mobility, and the necessary value systems.

Things will go wrong if, for whatever reason, a management generation starts interfering with this ratio of expansion. If times are hard and it is decided to sharply cut back recruitment for a number of years, then a severe price will be paid by the successors of the managers who made this decision. Twenty-five years later, those successors will sit around the table to choose new leaders. They will find out that the generation from which they have to select their successors is very thin in quality.

Things will go equally wrong if one corporate unit starts growing faster than the rest of the company. If recruitment must follow this growth, then the type of people recruited for that unit (engineers or accountants or physicists) will increase disproportionately in the total mix. Twenty-five years later, the company will find that it has lost diversity in its succession stream. Too many people speak the same language and agree too easily with one another. The company runs the risk of groupthink.

Entry-level recruitment should thus be seen not only as a vehicle for bringing in *new workers*. Twenty-five years from now, the quality of the seniormost leaders of the company will depend in part on the quality of the entry-level recruitment of today. This is particularly true in long-lived companies, which have demonstrated the value of promoting from within. James Collins and Jerry Porras, for example, report in their book *Built to Last* that "In seventeen hundred years of combined life spans across the visionary companies, we found only four incidents of going outside for a CEO—and those in only two companies."

In an economic company (a "puddle company"), recruitment simply means finding the right people to serve the asset base of the company. The pace of recruitment is handled by the numbers. If the company has more demand for its product than it has capacity, it admits new people (and machines). When demand slackens, the company reduces capacity by letting people go. At the same time, the people are defined in terms of skills: "We need 250 metal bashers" or "We have a surplus of paper pushers." The language of recruitment in economic companies betrays their underlying reasoning. It is not *people* who are hired or fired, but skills: "hands" to handle the machines or "brains" to make the right types of calculations.

In a "river company," by contrast, recruitment is a rite of passage. It represents the first moment for testing the fit between the new member and the community. This entry into the work community deserves, and receives, a lot of attention. It is as if people are being admitted to a club, a professional body (such as a medical association), or a trade union. New members must carry the right (professional) qualifications, but the harmony between the member and the institution is equally important. Do the values of the institution harmonize well with the values of the prospective new member?

In the spring, representatives of major corporations appear at the job markets at European universities. Only particular companies graze these academic meadows, because the cost (in managerial and recruiters' time) is high. But there is no other effective way to judge these very green graduates in terms of their potential for fitting well into a company. At Shell, recruiters do not simply look for computer specialists or people with a biochemistry background. We ask ourselves, about each candidate: "What's in there, inside that person? Where could I start him or her?" We ask them questions about their attitudes: "Are you prepared to work in other countries?" And we may show them our statement of business principles and ask if they're willing to adopt it.

The harmonization of values does not mean that the organization is looking for clones of its present membership. This would be dangerous, because it would stand in the way of acquiring the human diversity that is necessary for long-term survival. Looking for sympathetic clones at the moment of recruitment is one of the temptations that successful managers steel themselves to resist, difficult though that may be.

Even being critical and keeping our standards high, we will often have a choice among various candidates. That is the moment of risk. Having shortlisted the candidates on the basis of verifiable, more or less objective criteria, how are we going to make the final choice? We can only guess at the future of the human potential before us. So, we tend to select the recognizable. Anyone who seems vaguely "like me" or has a similar background is sympathetic. He or she, after all, will probably turn out more or less like *me*.

The risk is that going for the recognizable profile, the comfort of the known background, will reduce the diversity in the company's population. The diversity of people is probably already too narrow. It is the sign of a river company's maturity when managers begin to look for people who are *not* like themselves—who may come from a different ethnic or national background, for example, and will thus bring a new set of attitudes and talents to the corporate body.

## Development of People

And, in fact, the initial recruitment is only the first step. During the first two or three years, several of the new recruits depart. The company and the new person look at each other and decide that they don't, in fact, get along. They don't like each other. They don't fit.

But the majority of new recruits remains. In Shell, several hundred people per year remained worldwide during the 1980s. They were now recognized as members. They had entered into the system.

At any moment in time in any river company, there are at least three generations in place, poised to succeed each other.

- The generation of recruits, up through their early thirties, is continually ranked and rated by their supervisors and peers. There may be wild swings of approval and disapproval in these ratings: "Two years ago we thought Jeanne would make it up to managing director, but last year she was a bloody failure."
- Then, around the age of 37 to 40, the successive rankings of potential seem to stabilize. People enter the second generation, the generation of those in their late 30s and their 40s who are identified as high potential and exercise quite a bit of leadership in the company. (I was in this generation, for example, when I became a senior manager of Shell Brazil.)
- Finally, there are people in their fifties, the senior managers of the firm. (At Shell, the mandatory retirement age is 60.) They set the course of the company and should spend a great deal of time considering which people will succeed them.

This stream of succession does not imply a contract for life. Some members of the company will drop out or fail. But, after the first few years, the dropout rate becomes very low indeed. Moreover, those in the stream can feel confident that they will at least get a chance. And they know that the company will be willing to invest in their development.

A top manager needs to know that there will be a supply of good managers in the future. Look at the most brilliant planner, marketer, or production person in your operation. Where will his or her successor come from? It will take at least several years to grow such a person, and one or two more years to find them. An organization with an awareness of this problem will have an imperative to develop the human potential within the firm.

It might seem, at first glance, that a river company, with continuity, would not allow much movement of people through the enterprise.

But continuity *implies* movement. Over time, members are guided through the ranks in a process that aims at developing them up to their ultimate potential. To some extent this can be done through training, but it also requires a system of taking risks with people. Every time they take a new position, managers are, in effect, given another test about how far they could go. What is it that they could eventually do? What is the highest level at which they could effectively function? What aspect of their potential will be brought forth by this new position?

When I was a regional coordinator, I often had opportunities to conduct these tests. When a key position opened in, say, an operating company in Kenya or Brazil, I had to develop as clear an idea as possible of where this operating company was going. Where did we want it to go? Then I would look for a particular type of person—the person for whom this set of conditions would work as a tonic, calling forth capabilities that he or she never knew were there. If the position involved marketing in a growing market, I might not necessarily look for an experienced marketing manager. I might look for someone with the potential to get things done under pressure and arrange to send him or her to a three-week marketing course.

This type of development cannot be bought. It cannot even be developed as a program within one's own company. It can be produced only by taking risks and giving people time to come to fruition. When a new general manager of an operating company was appointed in my region, I would generally tell that person, "You can be reasonably sure of having this position for at least two years. Therefore, don't try to do too much in the first six months." I wanted them to give themselves time to learn in the position.

When managers get older, more creative efforts are needed to draw forth their potential. People in their forties, for example, often go through a crisis when they begin to see that their working life will end in less than two decades. They begin to wonder what they have done with their lives so far. At this stage, in a river company, they will often flourish with a transfer to another country or another function. The company shows them, in this fashion, that it doesn't consider them merely a specialized set of hands or brains, but a person with a continually expanding potential. They may have to come to terms with the fact that they will never be CEO or managing director, but the company has shown that it is important to keep their interest going and their involvement alive.

I required all my managers to spend at least 25 percent of their time on these types of issues related to the development and placement of the people who reported to them. General Electric CEO Jack Welch claims to require managers to spend 50 percent of their time on these sorts of development issues. Whatever the percentage of time you spend on it, this could be the most critical component of an executive's work.

## Assessing Human Potential

This emphasis on developing people also means that there must be reliable ways to evaluate the potential and performance of people—not to discipline them (for fear inhibits learning), but to better appreciate how to develop them.

A simplistic way to estimate ultimate potential is to ask the boss. Slightly more sophisticated methods include asking a succession of bosses, while the incumbent moves through the system. These methods are always unsatisfactory, because they rely on the opinion of a very few people.

The best way that I have seen took place at Royal Dutch/Shell. It consisted of assessments by ranking, once every two years, done by successive teams of people (usually the management team of the relevant business unit), the peers of the person being assessed, and a personnel officer. Because of the fast job rotation in the company, the composition of the team changed over the years. The result was that not only were people judged by a team (rather than being at the mercy of one person's opinion), but the team evolved through successive exercises.

This made the outcome much more acceptable to the incumbent, even if the ultimate potential was lower than he or she expected. Furthermore, the individual had the consolation of knowing that the exercise would be repeated every two years. An error made in one evaluation might be corrected the next time. Most important of all, however, was the way the continual shifting of evaluation allowed for a kind of ongoing human "flocking" (described in the next chapter), in which people continually came together to talk about the nature of human competence and capability.

## Trust and the Human Contract

In an economic company (a puddle company), there is an implicit underlying contract between the company and the individual. Often unwritten, it is nevertheless universally understood: the individual will deliver a skill in exchange for remuneration. This agreement is usually ratified under the umbrella of the country's social legislation or some collective labor agreement. It is based on the underlying premise that most people, in the end, really want economic reward—a higher paycheck—before all other goals.

Similarly, the river company has an underlying implicit contract. It, too, may never be written down, but it is obvious in every personnel decision made by the company. The individual will deliver care and commitment in exchange for the fact that the company will *try to develop each individual's potential to the maximum.*

I have already described some of the methods of this development. But its implications are equally important. Money is not considered a positive motivator in a river company. It is, as psychologist Abraham Maslow put it, a "negative hygiene factor." If money is insufficient, then people will grow dissatisfied, but *adding more money* (above the threshold of sufficient pay) will not motivate people to give more to the company. To give more, the individuals need to know that the community is interested in them as individuals, and they need to be interested themselves in the fate of the larger entity. To give more, both the entity and the individual need to care about each other.

Karl Weick, author of *The Social Psychology of Organizing*, has written that what people really want from the workplace is the "removal of equifinality," by which he meant that people want to see that they have brought order, design, and quality to the incoherent, ambiguous raw material of their work. They want to see that their decisions and efforts have had a positive impact. If they are treated only as "hands" or "brains," then they have no sense that they are removing equifinality, and they will look for it anywhere they can find it. They may concentrate on collective bargaining or getting a better salary—at least they can achieve that!—or they may go into secondary activities. They will become the local organizer for the Red Cross or run the cricket club. And that's a shame for their employer. Running a local cricket club is not easy, especially in terms of human relations. People who can do that effectively could accomplish a great deal for a company. The implicit contract of a river-company guarantees (not in words, but in actions) that they will have the opportunity to improve the world.

Robert Putnam, in his book on governance in democratic societies, makes the point that no amount of hierarchical discipline and power can possibly substitute for the absence of civic behavior and mutual trust in a community.[3] Once the main structure and its substructures (subsidiary companies, departments, individual members) agree that they have the same interests, goals, and purpose in life—once there is the conviction that everybody is better off staying together—then we have *true control*. The members of a community can be quite certain that all of them will try seriously to reach their common goals, without needing the waste, stress, and rigor of coercive discipline. I would go even further, to argue that a living company cannot abide coercive discipline. It will not last, at least in today's business environment, with those sorts of strict controls.

If that is true, then living companies absolutely depend on an implicit membership contract. Without the implicit contract, there is no guarantee of continuity. Without continuity, there can be no trust between the community and its individual members. Without trust there is no cohesion and, thus, no living company.

Consider, for example, some of the highly politicized situations where Shell managers have worked. During one of the turbulent periods before apartheid ended in South Africa, I went on a visit to the country. When I landed at the Johannesburg airport, I was greeted with a letter from the police. It said that if we asked questions *of our own executives* about our oil allocations while we were in South Africa, we would end up in jail. We could not check on the details of their supply system. We could rely only on trust.

This is an extreme example of an everyday dynamic. If you run a multinational company with operations in over 100 countries, there's only one way to run it. You cannot sit on the backs of your managers. You cannot send auditors every week. You must have mutual trust. Often decisions must be made in which the managers in that company have no time to check their decisions with superiors. They must move with the speed of basketball players, aiming with as clear an idea as possible of the company's goals, roaring across the court to reach those goals, an individual acting on behalf of a much larger entity that all of you comprise together.

Think of the ramifications if you can't trust people any more because they don't trust you, because they think you will throw them out to save ten dollars.

Without the mutual trust that comes from an implicit contract, the managers in the company will pay as much attention to their salaries and compensation as they will to the needs of the company. Therefore, there is much more probability of serious error simply because their attention has been diverted. Any basketball player can tell you that, if you take your eyes off the ball for even one-tenth of a second—for instance, if your eyes are continually diverted to the scoreboard—then you will lose points. If you do business at the $100 billion level, as in the Shell Group of companies, and your eye is diverted for one-tenth of a second, then you can put millions of dollars worth of activity in jeopardy.

Moreover, the implicit contract of the river company can accomplish miracles of profitability in its own right. We saw this at Shell in the early 1980s, when the turbulent new oil economy led us to construct a full-scale in-house commodities trading floor. When you have a commodities trading floor, you need commodities traders, and we did not know at first where we would find such people. Traders are very highly paid people. Their salaries soared far above the Shell remuneration scales. In the city of London, they were typically poached from other firms, and they could therefore be expected to be poached, in turn, from Shell. They did not fit at all into our human community.

We dealt with the problem, not by hiring traders, but by having people from the Shell community work as traders within the company—at salaries considerably lower than the city of London was paying. We could never have kept those people, even if they had formerly been Shell managers, by offering them the contract of an economic company. Some other company would have poached them. And, in fact, we lost some people, but far fewer than the salary differential might suggest. "With us," we could tell our trading managers, "you will be a trader only for two to three years. It will be a very useful experience, and from there you may well get promoted to marketing manager. We are interested in your long-term development." As we had with computer programmers in the late 1960s, when that skill demanded a premium, we undoubtedly paid traders a bit more than the Shell scales warranted, but we were still able to integrate them into the Shell system. This was very powerful. It even made the traders accept the idea that they would drive to work in a Ford Escort instead of a BMW.

Some companies do not institute an implicit river company contract because executives worry that they are creating sinecures. Is there not a danger, they ask, that people who have been managers for 20 or 30 years will regard their jobs as a license to coast? Indeed, that is a possibility. But at Shell, we found that the existence of an implicit contract allowed us to engage in regular dialogues about this. One manager can say to another, "I have doubts about your ability to pull your weight." And the first manager can respond by asking about the reasoning behind those doubts and contesting the impressions that led to them. Conversations like these can take place only in an atmosphere of mutual trust.

This implicit contract does not necessarily mean lifelong employment. The value systems of company and individual may turn out to be inharmonious. As an employee, you may decide that the company cannot help you meet your aspirations. Or the company may come to realize that every time someone succeeds you in a position, there is a mess to clean up, because you tend to choose quick solutions with unfortunate long-term consequences. More likely than not, after ten years, there will be no more career in this company for you; you have little potential left for this company to develop.

Nonetheless, the contract affirms that there is at least a statistical *probability* of lifetime employment. As an employee, you realize when signing on that there are no guarantees; you might be laid off at any point. But you also know that, statistically, you are likely to be valued for your experience, knowledge, and ability to produce results for the entity as a whole.

When people must be laid off, the implicit contract leads to a very different discussion than simply saying, "We're terribly sorry, but you have half a year to find another job." In a river company, a manager might say something like this: "Yes, the institution is in dire times, and we have to do something about it. One of the things we have to do (having taken some care to reshape our cost structure everywhere) is to eliminate some jobs, including yours. Having said this, we still have an implicit contract with you. Are there other ways to develop your potential that do not stand in the way of developing the potential of the company?"

## Outsiders

The implicit contract of a river company makes one think very carefully about the position of the outsiders who work, over the long term, in service to the company's purpose. This includes suppliers, distributors, franchisers, contractors, and even many customers—who are not included in the membership.

In these relationships, there is often a very clear understanding that, *for a limited period of time,* the company and the outsider will commit themselves to a relationship with each other. Joe Jaworski, for example, served as the head of the scenario team at Royal Dutch/Shell for three years. This put him in one of the most significant, most visible roles at Shell Center, the headquarters of the global group of companies. As he entered into that activity, Joe became a fully accepted full-time member, a "we" member of the team. But everyone concerned knew that, at the end of his tenure, that relationship would end. For these types of relationships to work, there must be a special state of commitment, the sort of mutual concern *without* formal structure, that Joe writes about in his book *Synchronicity.*[4]

There are many such middle-ground positions. The details differ.

For example, someone in that position might not get a pension, but they might get an added payment which allows them to develop their own pension contract. The important thing is that the contract exists, that it is two-sided—both parties must consciously think about it and accept it—and that it recognizes the value of the two entities, the contractor and the company, to each other.

Outsiders are very important to a river company. With its required recruitment policies, it cannot meet capacity shortfalls by recruiting more members. Immediate capacity needs should be met by subcontracting resources from the outside world. This form of handling personnel matters is increasingly common. In Italy, Benetton handles only a minor part of its manufacturing with its own people; all but 20 percent is subcontracted. Relatively few members are admitted to the inner core of the work community.

Some businesspeople fear that, by contracting out the physical operations of their business, they may lose control or become more vulnerable to takeover or imitation by competitors. This fear is not entirely unfounded, but it deserves a closer look.

The Shell Group runs one of the world's biggest commercial operations with "only" about 110,000 people. But the number of people working on Shell projects is far greater. Shell performs very few of the necessary operations by itself. Shell's people do not drill the wells, lay the pipelines, build the refineries, or transport most of the oil. The vast majority of Shell's retail outlets remain in the hands of independent operators. Shell itself is mostly a management club. Members of Shell's work community have a unique ability: to get any operation going, anywhere in the world with most of the physical work handled by independent companies. This job—combining internal and external operations into a productive whole—is more difficult to execute *and* to imitate than if Shell people handled every job themselves.

We saw evidence of this during the spate of nationalizations of the oil industry in the 1970s. National governments, with varying levels of technical sophistication, took over oilfields and refineries. We consoled ourselves at Shell by saying that they could not manage these assets as well as we could. That was probably true. Nonetheless, none of the nationalizations went so far off track that they had to be reversed (although some countries were clever enough to let the original owners run the oilfields and refineries). The truth is that it is nearly always possible to hire somebody to run an asset like a refinery or an oilfield.

The only nationalizations that were reversed were *marketing* companies in a few South American and African countries. This work involved distributing our sophisticated product to logistically difficult places—and making sure that they got paid for the delivery. Local transporters, resellers, and storage handled most of the physical work, so the local governments (and we) assumed it would be the easiest job to take over. It was the hardest. The government of Argentina could not learn to fit together an activity that brought high-specification jet fuel to an airport in Buenos Aires, gasoline to a petrol depot near Bariloche, and motor lubricant to a store in Rio Gallegos, in the right quantities at the right costs and at the right time. Only a work community with a highly trained, coherent membership and high levels of learning can handle a job like that: a job managing outsiders.

## Exit Rules

The need for rules about continuity is important not only when people enter the community, but when they exit in retirement. Exit rules, for example, stipulate that there is a fixed moment of retirement for each and every member—without exception. At Shell, for example, all managers leave the company at age 60. River companies are the opposite of that old cartoon that shows 12 geriatric board members nodding slowly to the chairman, who is proposing to extend the retirement age by one more year!

Strict exit rules require the incumbent management to recognize that they are there for only a limited amount of time. Leadership becomes stewardship. Just as you took over from somebody, you will hand your leadership over to somebody else. Your legacy at the company will depend on whether you kept the shop as healthy as you found it or made it just a bit healthier. Strict exit rules are thus good for humility.

Of course, the rule-enforced departure is seldom without a little tension, but an exit from a river company is not felt as a personal defeat. On the contrary, many alumni of Shell and other companies find good use of their knowledge in academia, statesmanship, or consulting. Consolation prizes, such as "honorary jobs," should be avoided; elephants' graveyards are pathetic places.

## When a River Company Changes Course

And what of premature exit—when people are forced to leave the company before they wish and before they have reached retirement age? That, to me, is a symptom of a deeper problem. If a river company seems to suddenly turn on a dime and traumatically begin to lay off people in violation of the implicit community contract, then this is a signal. The river company is trying to become a "puddle." It is being turned into an economic company.

In my present capacity as an adviser, I frequently find myself in meetings these days at companies that have made this shift. I have learned to recognize the mood in such a company. It is understood, for the first time, that only a few dozen people, at very senior levels, are the true "members of the company." Everyone else is subject to performance evaluations, with their jobs at risk.

Sometimes I sit at lunch, or in a meeting, with managers who have recently found themselves moved into that second group—the people at risk. The mood in these meetings is invariably somber, with a palpable sense of insecurity. Most of them are not *really* at risk; they know that their skills are valued enough that they will remain employed, at least for the moment. But they do not have the assurance that they once had, the assurance that the organization is concerned about their development. Their future with the company is on the line. Perhaps one day they might be reelected into membership, someday, but even then, there would be a scar—a memory of the time when they had not been selected to belong.

Often, in these meetings, it takes half an hour or more for people to start talking about their problems and ideas. In the old days, they rarely needed more than a minute or two before engaging each other.

But now they are not working for the community any more. They are simply working for themselves.

Other times I meet with managers who have been selected for the elite, the people whose membership is secure. The atmosphere at these meetings is ebullient; it evokes the same feelings of camaraderie ("us with a capital *U*") and identification with the whole that had existed throughout the organization in the past. There is, of course, a bitter-sweet awareness of the people who have been laid off, and the conversation often regretfully turns to the circumstances that have made this move necessary.

"What are you going to do," I sometimes ask at these meetings, "about the people who will *stay?* How will they make sure that the people remaining, throughout the organization, recognize that they are still members of the company? How will they make people feel that their identity is valued as part of the whole?"

I often find that the thought hasn't even entered their minds. In many cases, the management team's thinking has been focused on the people who will be laid off. How will they make their selection of who goes and who stays? What will the company say to the trade union? How will they treat the "downsized" people in terms of severance pay or helping them get another job? There is rarely much thought left for the people who remain. Implicitly, the message of the company to those people is this: "You may stay, but it does not necessarily mean that you are still a member."

In those circumstances, what happens to trust? What happens to the resilience that the company needs in its managers? What happens to productivity, to discipline, and to the company's capabilities as a whole?

It takes a long time to build a river company. But if you have a river company in place, you can demolish it in less than 12 months. Simply follow these easy steps:

1. Declare that the company isn't profitable enough. Henceforth, your goal will be a specific amount of return on capital employed.
2. Develop an action plan in which all assets will be trimmed back across the board to meet these goals.
3. Follow the plan.

History shows that many companies that go this route face repercussions after a year or two. Exxon let 15,000 people go in 1986, in the wake of the oil price collapse. They concentrated power in a narrow chain of command and took away one side of their organizational matrix structure. In the process, they considerably reduced their managerial capacity. A year later, the Valdez oil spill incident took place. It took them 48 hours to react. That 48 hours has so far cost them $3 billion in cleanup costs, bad publicity, and legal fees. And the ticker is still counting.

For a while, it was difficult to find Exxon people with whom to conduct business. Shell has a 50-50 partnership with Exxon in a North Sea operation. Both sides meet regularly in joint project groups and operating committees, asking, "We are thinking of doing this or that in a certain way. What do you think?" Suddenly, it was difficult to find people at Exxon who would answer these questions. They would no longer stick their necks out. They no longer seemed confident of their relationship with the parent company, and their ability to take constructive risks had been destroyed.

At another company, which had lost a great deal of people suddenly, a manager told me this: "From one day to the next, our productivity decreased by 15 percent. People come to the office and go to the coffee machine right away. They spend the first hour out of the day asking what they can do today for themselves."

Senior managers who inadvertently turn river companies into economic companies are not willfully destructive. They are simply trying to do their best against the background of a widespread misapprehension of corporate purpose. They are struggling with a terrible dilemma. When shareholders and outside regulatory bodies ask about the senior managers' results, they do not ask about efforts to improve community. They do not inquire about the company's prospects for a long and prosperous existence. They ask, "What is your return on capital employed? Aren't you overcapitalized?" and "What is your productivity?"

Being seen by the outside world as "managers of capital assets" places an almost irresistible pull on some river companies, despite the internal needs to build and maintain a human work community. It is understandable that these companies evolve, more or less quickly, into companies that are like puddles. Top managers are pulled by the outside world in one direction and by the needs of the work community in the other.

To manage a corporation effectively, we must learn how to treat institutions as living ecosystems—set up with the recognition that they will live or die according to the same natural laws that govern human growth and development. As we will see in the next chapter, this sort of management does not take place primarily in the arenas of information systems and reengineering. It is a social matter. It has to do with providing opportunities for managers to learn together.

# ECOLOGY

# 7

# Flocking

ACCORDING TO THE *CONCISE OXFORD DICTIONARY*, ECOLOGY IS the branch of biology dealing with the relationships between organisms and their surroundings, including other organisms.

I first learned about ecology in organizations during a visit with Allan Wilson, a zoologist/biochemist based at the University of California at Berkeley. I had come to Wilson only by happenstance; Peter Schwartz, then the head of our scenario team at Group Planning, heard a reference to him during a trip to California. Peter thought that Wilson's work might complement our other investigations into accelerating learning.[1]

Wilson's work in evolutionary biology would gain him the MacArthur "genius" prize several years later, but at that time, we knew him only as someone who studied the way animals learned. He knew just as little about us. Indeed, he was bemused to find a trio of Royal Dutch/Shell planners knocking on his door one morning. Clearly, he was not used to businesspeople showing an interest in his work—let alone managers from a multinational oil company. So we explained, as best we could, that we were trying to understand the nature of learning in large organizations like our own. We thought there might be a clue in the nature of learning among animals.

"Ah, well, then . . . ," Professor Wilson said. He was not sure that his work was relevant to ours, but he was quite happy to tell us about the role of learning in the evolution of life. We then passed a fascinating couple of hours in which he told us, in much-simplified language, about the "genetic clock" embedded in the molecules of genes of all species. The molecules of genetic material, he said, change at a surprisingly constant rate in the evolution of organisms, even those whose anatomy is evolving at very different rates. Through biochemical analysis of genetic material, it was possible to measure each species for the number of genetic "ticks" that it had undergone to reach its current state. Although not all his colleagues subscribed to the idea, Allan Wilson was convinced that the genetic clock runs at the same rate in every living organism, even in bacteria. A species with more ticks of the genetic clock in its structure would have evolved further than a species with fewer ticks.

"Do you understand," Professor Wilson asked us, "that in this way it is possible to establish a table of all the species on Earth, and see who would come out as the 'most evolved'?"

Yes, surely we understood.

"Well, then," he said, "you would not be surprised to hear which species was number one—the most evolved species on earth."

No, indeed, we would not be surprised. And, indeed, the most highly evolved was the human species.

"But what about number two?" asked Wilson. "Which species, genus, or family is the *second* most evolved?"

The Shell executives could not guess. It turned out, Wilson said, that number two in the evolutionary race, at least as highly evolved as the higher primates, were members of the bird family. Songbirds, in particular, show a high rate of anatomical evolution. "Isn't that surprising?" he asked.

Why would it be surprising?

"Because the common ancestor of all birds is, in evolutionary terms, a relative newcomer. Birds evolved out of the reptile family. They had little time to reach the evolutionary level where they are nowadays. It is especially surprising if we think of evolution in terms of a Darwinian battle of survival and selection through the generations."

Conventional natural selection theory, he told us, posited that the only changes occurred between generations, as successful individuals reproduced more frequently and the new generation carried forward the most successful genes. But that theory could not account for the songbirds. They had simply had too little time to evolve to their current number of ticks on the molecular clock. There had not been a sufficient number of generations. How come, then, during a given time scale, one species (like the songbirds) seemed to have evolved so much further than others?

Could something else happen *during* the life of a generation that accelerated the evolution of that species? That question was the focus of Allan Wilson's current research. He had developed a hypothesis about "intergenerational learning"—that species behavior, rather than environmental change, was the major driving force for evolution. In other words, certain species evolved "faster," according to the ticks on the molecular clock, because they exhibited a particular type of behavior.

And what behavior did primates and songbirds share, to put them at the top of the table of evolved species? Wilson theorized that accelerated anatomical evolution took place in species with three particular characteristics:

- **Innovation.** Either as individuals or as a community, the species has the capacity (or at least the potential) to invent new behavior. They can develop skills that allow them to exploit their environment in new ways.

- **Social propagation.** There is an established process for transmission of a skill from the individual to the community as a whole—not genetically, but somehow through direct communication.

- **Mobility.** The individuals of the species have the ability to move around, and (more importantly) they actually use it! They flock or move in herds, rather than sitting in isolated territories.

## The Titmouse and the Milk Bottle

To test this hypothesis, Wilson had turned to a well-documented case involving the British titmouse, a small songbird common in English gardens. The United Kingdom has a longstanding milk distribution system in which milkmen in small trucks bring the milk in bottles to the door of each country house. At the beginning of this century, these milk bottles had no top. Birds had easy access to the cream which settled in the top of the bottle. Two different species of British garden birds, the titmice and the red robins, learned to siphon up cream from the bottles and tap this new, rich food source.

This *innovation,* in itself, was already quite an achievement. But it also had evolutionary effect. The cream was much richer than the usual food sources of these birds, and the two species underwent some adaptation of their digestive systems to cope with the unusual nutrients. This internal adaptation almost certainly took place through Darwinian selection.

Then, between the two world wars, the UK dairy distributors closed access to the food source by placing aluminum seals on the bottles.

By the early 1950s, the entire titmouse population of the UK—about a million birds—had learned how to pierce the aluminum seals. Regaining access to this rich food source provided an important victory for the titmouse family as a whole; it gave them an advantage in the battle for survival. Conversely, the red robins, as a family, never regained access to the cream. Occasionally, an individual robin learns how to pierce the seals of the milk bottles, but the knowledge never passes to the rest of the species.

In short, the titmice went through an extraordinarily successful institutional learning process. The red robins failed, even though individual robins had been as innovative as individual titmice. Moreover, the difference could not be attributed to their ability to communicate. As songbirds, both the titmice and the red robins had the same wide range of means of communication: color, behavior, movements, and song. The explanation, said Professor Wilson, could be found only in the *social propagation* process: the way titmice spread their skill from one individual to members of the species as a whole.

In spring, the titmice live in couples until they have reared their young. By early summer, when the young titmice are flying and feeding on their own, we see the birds moving from garden to garden in flocks of eight to ten individuals. These flocks seem to remain intact, moving together around the countryside, and the period of *mobility* lasts for two to three months.

Red robins, by contrast, are territorial birds. A male robin will not allow another male to enter its territory. When threatened, the robin sends a warning, as if to say, "Keep the hell out of here." In general, red robins tend to communicate with each other in an antagonistic manner, with fixed boundaries that they do not cross.

Birds that flock, said Allan Wilson, seem to learn faster. They increase their chances to survive and evolve more quickly.

## Flocking in Organizations

Any organization with several hundred people is bound to have at least a couple of innovators. There are always people curious enough to poke their way into new discoveries, like the titmice finding their cream. However, keeping a few innovators on hand is not enough, in itself, for institutional learning. The organization must leave *space* for them, so that they do not feel squelched and their innovations have time to develop. (This is the purpose of such well-known innovations as the "skunkworks" of Lockheed Aircraft—spaces set aside for innovators to work without interference from the rest of the organization. It also raises deeper issues of control and freedom, to which we will return at the end of this chapter.)

Even if you develop a high-caliber system of innovation, you will *still* not have institutional learning until you develop the ability to "flock." Flocking depends on two of Allan Wilson's key criteria for learning: *mobility* of people and some effective mechanism of *social transmission*.

Consider, for example, the most effective possible forms of training and development. Some managers see conventional training and development as merely an opportunity to acquire some new skills. However, if it is given the wider definition of "developing individuals up to their potential" (as discussed in Chapter 6, "Managing for Profit or for Longevity"), then training and development becomes a powerful vehicle for institutionalizing learning. Over time, the capabilities of the organization as a whole increase, more than you would expect merely from summing together the increase in individuals' capabilities.

What qualities must this training have to be effective? First, it must encourage *mobility*. At Shell, for instance, executive development programs run parallel to a person's career. The organization spends about U.S. $2,400 per employee each year on education; half represents the pure cost of five to six days' training, and the other half consists of the trainees' salaries.[2] As always with training, whereas the costs are substantial and quantifiable, the results cannot be measured. But the intangible results are undeniable: Shell people know that, at every stage of their career, they will be encouraged to move forward or to move into new endeavors or to bring themselves (and the company) new skills.

Even more significantly, most of the training they undergo is collaborative and related to real-world activities. Managers from all over the world meet in collaborative problem-solving exercises, so that the firm is constantly improving its own capabilities, even during "time-out" periods for education.

I have found it very important for teams of disparate people to undergo intensive training together at regular intervals. Apart from knowledge transfer, such an intensive training program brings together many groups of people, learners and trainers, all from the same corporation, but coming from very different cultural backgrounds and many different professional and academic disciplines. The flocking is intensive; course attendees nearly always tell you afterwards, "It was not so much what I learned in the official sessions, but what I picked up from my colleagues during the breaks that was important."

As with the titmouse's innovation, when it learned to siphon cream from English milk bottles, a well-designed program of development can have evolutionary effect. The innovation spreads rapidly through the organization, without being *commanded* to spread. Somehow, people just seem to know what to do. They gain and spread the knowledge because they have been given structures that encourage flocking.

## Job Mobility

One question often pops up in debates among human relations and human resources managers: Should people be thoroughly trained to do a particular job and, once they have learned to do it more or less decently, left in place so that they provide a return on the investment of their training, or should we move people around many jobs during their career and let them accumulate experience?

Although the two approaches to job rotation are not necessarily in contradiction (one can move people around and still train them thoroughly for each job), the philosophy underlying each is quite different. The first approach is analytical; it sees the company as a combination of machines and labor, organized to produce the highest possible proceeds at minimum costs. The organization is positioned to gain the most value possible from its investment in the "asset" of "human capital."

The second approach sees the company as a self-perpetuating work community. Each employee has an ultimate potential, and it is in the company's interests to help the individual reach that potential. Thus, people move from job to job, within the enterprise—in part so they accumulate the maximum experience available during a working life and in part so that, through "flocking," the organization gains from their experiences.

The military in many countries has long learned the advantages of mobility. Promotion by merit allows the creation of a top command level from a much wider recruitment base in the population. It considerably increases the chances of having a more capable officer corps. Today's general is not necessarily the son of yesterday's general. A lifelong emphasis on training—from officers' schools to continual learning for enlisted soldiers—is also a key component in achieving this end.

## Social Propagation

Does mobility mean only that you move as an individual, from group to group? Or can it also involve groups and teams that move from situation to situation?

It probably means both.

Most innovative companies are run by teams. This is because teams have a higher capacity to learn than individuals. In fact, in most companies with a certain degree of complexity, most decisions are made by teams.

The capacity for a management team's learning is influenced by the way the team is defined. It should include all the people (directly or indirectly) who together *have the power to act* on their common interest. Ideally, a management team at any level of the company should include all people who are necessary for the implementation of that team's decisions. They should be able to work together on common problems, each with his or her individual contribution and technical specialty. This would be an ideal "flock."

Some companies facilitate flocking of their management teams; other companies have stronger territorial tendencies. They classify members by their specialty, skill, or mandate—production engineers in one "function," marketers in another. Then they appoint a management team of people from various functions and give each a specific written statement, spelling out in detail exactly what their assignment should be. Each member is carefully instructed to avoid encroaching on the others' territories; marketing people do not oversee production, and production people steer clear of marketing concerns. Finance managers concern themselves with measurement and money handling, and do not permit themselves to get involved in process concerns, while process managers ignore the imperatives of finance, except where they are given direct orders. Each red robin is allocated his or her territory in the corporate garden.

We should therefore not be surprised, when these teams communicate as antagonistically as red robins, at squabbling at the boundaries of their territories. The amount of institutional learning is limited.

As in bird species, the resulting social transmission will be different in a territorial company. Both the territorial and the flocking company may employ equally innovative individuals, but the chances that the innovative ideas will become company policy are much reduced in the territorial company.

A caveat, however, is necessary. Flocking is hard-wired into the titmouse species. Robins cannot be trained to flock; flocking is not part of their genetic makeup. Therefore, anyone who tries to apply this metaphor literally might be tempted to argue that companies, too, are genetically predetermined. Some cultures are like songbirds: they can learn to flock more easily because they have institutional learning bred into them, whereas other companies are more like mollusks. In that case, it's hardly worth trying, because the capacity for learning is innate and unchangeable . . . isn't it?

I doubt it. Surely, corporate life is not a Greek tragedy in which the outcome is hard-wired into the characters by the Olympian gods, and the play can climax only in its inevitable tragic ending. Human organizations have resources for evolution, as we will see in later chapters, that songbirds do not. And, even if they have not participated in designing a company from its birth, many managers will find themselves in a position with influence on some part of the business. From there, they can begin to remodel the company's structures and policies in a way that facilitates flocking and improves the company's ability to learn.

## Innovation and the Dilemma of Freedom

Many managers shrink from institutional learning. They fear flocking, and they are terrified of innovation. And they are quite right to feel this way. They are stuck on the horns of the age-old managerial dilemma between control and freedom.

Innovation and flocking require *organizational space*—freedom from control, from direction, and from punishment for failures. Experiments must take place with relative safety. Conversation must be free and candid, without fear of reprisal. Employee movements must be largely self-determined; no one can "command" a bird to flock in a

certain direction, because the travel pattern of the flock emerges from
its own movement.

This is terrain where many managers fear to tread. In many companies, creating space is seen by most managers as losing efficiency, or
even losing cohesion. It is not a simple matter to decide, one Monday
morning, "We are going to create an atmosphere of space in this company." Having made that decision, you lie awake at night. God knows
what some idiot is doing this very moment, you think, in Malaysia or
Chile or Sweden—or in your own office.

Because the worry is so agonizing, the average manager is inclined
to err on the side of control. A restful night's sleep is a very compelling
motive. In the process, however, the organization's ability to flock is
compromised.

Just as a car buyer expects a new car to behave in a known and
predictable way, a manager wants a company to produce predictable
results and to give timely warnings when it is running on a dangerous
course. Both car buyer and manager require an acceptable degree of
control before they will entrust their lives (literally or metaphorically)
to their new vehicle. This need for control is so fundamental that it has
dominated management literature for 100 years. Books abound on financial control systems and on organizational theory for effective managerial control. The apogee came in the 1950s, with Taylorism, "scientific management," and the widespread adoption of time-and-motion
studies. Companies, these mixtures of people and capital assets, were
reduced to machines. Managers were reduced to being machinists. The
search for total control, however, could not be sustained. The cost of
maintaining a company without flocking and innovation, where every
adaptation had to be ordered from the highest levels of the hierarchy,
was too great.

Nowadays most managers recognize that cost. Almost everyone is
in favor of decentralization and empowerment—in other words, for increasing freedom. But even today, few dare to risk the accompanying
loss of control.

Most of those who dare will show their fears in a crisis. They will
recentralize quickly, pulling power back into the center and into the
top. After all, beneath the rhetoric about "empowerment," most man-

agers trust themselves infinitely more than they trust anybody else. They will have to live or die with the consequences.

This dilemma, as it happens, is very common in ecological matters. To behave with ecological concern often requires a leap of faith: that you will be better protected by harmony and flocking than by territoriality and force of will.

Ecology, after all, is itself a process of Piaget's learning through accommodation. Learning in ecosystems takes place constantly, as entities adapt themselves to new understandings, based on changing conditions in their environment. The entities that survive in a turbulent ecosystem are those that can adapt themselves to new understandings, based on changing conditions in their environment.

Thus, what sorts of qualities would position an entity well for this sort of learning? Would it be better to be strong and stalwart, to dominate a niche? Or would entities, like companies, do well to cultivate more modest, adaptive qualities, such as tolerance and an appreciation of internal space?

# 8

# The Tolerant Company

ROSE GARDENERS IN A TEMPERATE CLIMATE FACE A CHOICE
every spring: how to prune our roses. More than any other single factor under our control, the long-term fate of a rose garden depends on
this decision.

This choice, in turn, depends on the result you want to achieve that
summer. If you want to have the largest and most glorious roses of the
neighborhood, you will prune hard. You will reduce each rose plant to
a maximum of three stems. Each of these stems will be limited to three
buds. Everything but those nine strongest buds will be clipped away, to
get the maximum results: the biggest rose. This represents a policy of
low tolerance and tight control. You force the plant to make the maximum use of its available resources, by putting them into the rose's
"core business." You may expect, in June, to see some sizable flowers
with which to dazzle the neighbors.

However, if this is an unlucky year, you might get a severe night
frost in late April or early May. Then your rose plants may well suffer
serious damage to the limited number of shoots that remain after your
pruning. If the frost is serious, or if deer visit, or if there is a sudden in-

vasion of green fly, you may not get any roses at all this year. You may lose the main stems or the whole plant! Pruning hard is a dangerous policy in an unpredictable environment.

Thus, if you know that you live in a spot where nature may play tricks on you, and if your primary desire is to maintain your roses, year after year, you may opt for a policy of high tolerance. You will leave more stems on the plant and more buds on each stem. You may even leave some buds that seem, at first glance, like they might produce distinctly *un*spectacular roses.

You will never have the biggest roses in the neighborhood, but you have a much-enhanced chance of having roses every year. You also achieve a gradual renewal of the plant. By leaving young, weaker shoots on the plant, you give them the chance to grow and to strengthen, so that they can take over the task of the main shoots in a couple of years' time. In short, a tolerant pruning policy achieves two ends:

- It makes it easier to cope with unexpected environmental changes.
- It leads to a continuous, gradual restructuring of the plant.

This policy of tolerance admittedly wastes resources. As they grow, the extra buds drain away nutrients and energy from the main stem of the plant. But in an unpredictable environment, this policy of tolerance makes the rose healthier. It allows the rose and the environment to continually engage each other, without endangering the rose's permanent growth. Tolerance of internal weakness, ironically enough, allows the rose to be stronger in the long run.

Questions of tolerance are a fundamental part of a company's ecological stance. Ecology does not only concern the relationship between a company and its surroundings. Equally important are the company's relationships with the different personae inside itself: its individual members, its subsidiary companies, and its branches. To tolerate a variety of life forms within oneself gives a company the resilience to withstand stress and even disaster.

## Decentralization and Tolerance

We saw this in our Shell study about corporate survivors. Long-lived companies, we concluded, were tolerant. However, at the time, we did not talk about "tolerance" or "adaptability." Instead, we used the terms *decentralization* and *diversification*. Companies that had managed to survive for a long time, we wrote, had done so by letting things happen in the margin: allowing activities outside the core business to be set up by not coming down like a ton of bricks on every diversion in which local people seem to believe fervently:

> [The companies] have made full use of decentralized structures and delegated authorities. The companies have not insisted upon a relevance to the original business as a criterion for selecting new business possibilities nor upon a central control over moves to diversify.[1]

Every company we found that had been in existence for 100 years or more had gone through a period of adaptation so profound that it had had to thoroughly alter its core business portfolio. Some had made this change several times:

- Booker McConnell, the "Guyanese company," was a British company formed in 1900. Its first business was sugar production in South America. It then began spreading its investments, under an outward-oriented management, in anticipation of the nationalization of its original core business. It moved into shopkeeping and shipping, as well as into publishing (through an "Authors Division"). Its annual Booker prize for literature is famous, although Booker McConnell's corporate identity remains largely unknown.
- W. R. Grace, founded in 1854 by an Irish immigrant in Peru, traded in guano (a natural fertilizer). Then it moved into sugar and tin. Ultimately, the company established Pan American Airways. Today, it is primarily a chemical company, although it is also the leading U.S. provider of kidney dialysis services.[2]
- In 1590 an ancestor of the Sumitomo family named Riemon Soga

opened a copper casting shop in Kyoto. From copper casting, Sumitomo moved into trading and then, in the seventeenth century, into mining. In the nineteenth century, the company developed a strong manufacturing orientation. Nowadays, it is composed of 15 main companies which include banking and chemical businesses.

To be sure, most of these changes involved some sort of crisis that affected the entire organization, from its roots to its far-flung branches. But, from what we can tell, for the people running the enterprises at the time these changes were probably far more gradual than we would guess. Some of them might have been almost imperceptible from the outset, even from the inside. All of them were accomplished without losing the company's corporate identity or having the company subsumed by another organization.

As I pondered the link between this decentralization and corporate longevity, I reflected that these companies had developed their values and organizational principles during the seventeenth, eighteenth, nineteenth, and early twentieth centuries—long before words like *decentralization* and *diversification* had even entered common usage. How had they described their own policies to themselves? What did the leaders, owners, and managers of centuries past think about their own efforts to build internal hardiness through diversity and openness?

I do not know how *they* would have described it, but the question led me to understand it more completely in my own mind. Companies such as Booker McConnell, W. R. Grace, and Sumitomo—as well as others such as DuPont, Mitsui, and Stora—found it easier to adapt because they had *tolerance*. Tolerance was the core quality that made it possible to diversify and decentralize, yet still manage the entity as a whole. These companies were particularly tolerant of activities in the margin: small, seemingly strange businesses that might have been pruned off the corporate rosebush elsewhere, but here were given enough resources to straggle along until the corporation needed them as an outlet for endeavor.

When a DuPont needed to move into chemicals; a Sumitomo, into banking; or a W. R. Grace, into aviation, there was already a budding nexus of capability within the enterprise, ready to move into a new status as a core business. Moreover, because the company had been tolerant of this "bud" of new activity, it had been given time and room to emerge organically from the core structure. Thus its presence *in itself* demonstrated where the corporate entity as a whole might naturally and profitably move next.

In short, systems that deliberately introduce diversity into the product line—even at the expense of short-term proceeds—and allow activities to go on undisturbed in the margin of the field, have greatly enhanced chances of survival across the generations. These systems are tolerant. Tolerant systems survive.

At first glance, tolerance of diversity might seem to contradict the need for cohesion. But, as we noted in Chapter 6, "Managing for Profit or for Longevity," cohesion itself is improved by diversity. Royal Dutch/Shell is stronger *because* of the differences between Deutsche Shell and Shell Brazil, not *in spite* of them. The differences between the operating companies has forced strength into the global parent; it must be a strong enough container to hold all of those differences without cracking. This strength has been built up gradually, over time. It is made possible by the fact that the individual goals of the substructures (the operating companies) are harmonious with and best served by the goals of the higher-level system. At the same time, full use can be made of the wealth of diversity that is available in the system as a whole.

In addition, a cohesive system must be open to change and diversity. Tolerance is a measure of the *openness* of a system. The more tolerant a company, the more new people and ideas it can absorb and foster over time. Tolerance is a dynamic characteristic; it changes the composition of the company. Diverse people, products, and ideas require us to be patient with them; indeed, tolerance *is* patience. It requires time.

At the moment, as it happens, the prevailing managerial attitudes tend to discount the value of tolerance. Small, budding businesses in the margin are not seen as an organizational asset. During the 1970s, many corporations learned that diversification is a dangerous route to take. The lessons were so painful that we are still in a long period of reaction, an antidiversification movement that has already lasted 20 years. "Stick to your knitting," we are told. "Go back to basics." Managers concentrate on their "core competencies" and "core businesses."

They eliminate all businesses that do not perform first or second in their markets. Yet, amid these fashionable attitudes, there are strong indications that, in order to survive in an age of technological, political, economic, and social upheavals, a company must be able to change the emphasis of its business portfolio completely. There may be a "core competency" at any given moment, but in the next moment, a new core competency may be needed.

Why, then, was the last round of diversification so devastating? During the 1960s and 1970s, most of it took place by dictum. Diversifications were initiated from a central control point at the top of the firm. They were financed through great allocations of "new business" investment.

By contrast, the long-term corporate survivors we had studied at Shell had made their changes in gradual, incremental ways—almost always in anticipation of customer needs. New business was not required to be relevant to the original business, and, above all, there was no central control over the diversifications. They were often minimally financed or self-financing; often, they were simply the natural result of letting some group of inventors or creators within the firm have time to experiment and take risks.

Historically, *diversification by tolerance* for activities in the margin has a much better track record than *diversification by dictum*. Could it be, in fact, that the very top of a company is not the best place to take initiatives—except in a crisis? Under "normal" conditions, to judge by the record of long-lived companies, the senior manager of a company should make fewer decisions about the business itself and spend that time instead focused on creating conditions in which other people within the company can make good decisions about the business.

Tolerance, in other words, is derived from a value system. It can only exist in a company where people recognize the value of creating space for innovation. This is the reason why some companies set aside pockets of innovation: the "skunkworks" of Lockheed, or the famous sidelines at 3M and Motorola, which grew into main lines of business. In essence, these companies are creating pockets of organizational space in which innovation can emerge. The pockets tend to be hidden away in backwaters of the company. The senior managers trust them, don't oversee them, keep them generally out of sight and out of mind, and don't worry about them—until they are needed.

## The Parable of the Chilean Potato

A few years after the Shell study was finished, I mentioned some of its findings and the thoughts it called forth in my mind at a dinner party in San Francisco. Paul Hawken, author of *The Next Economy,* was one of the other guests, and he told me the story of the Chilean potato.

There was a time, he said, when the balance of payments of Chile deteriorated to the point that foreign exchange became a problem to the country. The causes seemed clear: Chile could no longer produce its own food and had to rely increasingly on imports. The United States decided to offer a helping hand and dispatched a team of agronomists to study the problem.

The team flew to Santiago de Chile and proceeded from there directly to the Andes Mountains. The Andes are the region where the potato originated; it is still a main staple in the Chilean diet. Potatoes have grown for thousands of years at considerable heights in the mountains.

The U.S. agronomists climbed these heights and looked at the potato fields. The fields clung precipitously to the mountainsides. They had highly irregular shapes and were interspersed with boulders. Within each field, the agronomists discovered ten or more varieties of potatoes growing. There were round potatoes and elongated potatoes; red, white, and blue potatoes; and—more perturbing to the scientists— some plants that bore many potatoes and others that bore only a few tubers. This seemed terribly inefficient.

Came harvesting time and the insights of the agricultural aid team increased even more. They noticed that the peasants were less than systematic—almost "lazy"—in the way they reaped the crop. A considerable number of plants in the nooks and corners of the oddly shaped fields were overlooked and left to grow wild. By then the team had most of the elements needed to write a convincing report. Out came the hand-held computers. The calculations showed, beyond doubt, that a more careful selection of seed potatoes, a switch to higher-yield varieties, and a more systematic weeding and cropping of the fields would increase the annual crop by at least 15 percent. Because this equaled the shortfall in the country's food production, the team took their plane back to the United States with the feeling of a job well done.

But the advice was wrong. However scientific the agronomists' approach may have been, they could not compete with the accumulated local experience, based on thousands of years of potato growing in the Andes.

Chilean peasants, based all their lives in the mountains, know that a wide variety of terrible things could harm their potatoes. There may be a late night frost in spring, or a caterpillar plague in summer. Mildew might destroy the plants before any tubers have formed, or winter might come too early. Over the years, each of these calamities has taken place from time to time.

Whenever a new calamity strikes, the peasants walk up to their fields and look everywhere—in the corners, behind the boulders, and amid the weeds—for the surviving potato plants. Only these surviving plants are immune to the latest plague. At harvesting time the peasants will carefully dig up the survivors and take the precious potato tubers back to their huts. They and their children may have to go through a winter of famine, but at least they have next year's seed potatoes from which a new start can be made. They are not locked into a particular set of farming practices, or a particular type of potato; they may be inefficient at times, but they have diversity *bred into their everyday practice,* diversity that allows them to meet unforeseen disaster.

Paul's story about the Chilean potatoes illustrated, to me at least, that tolerance toward the margin is a generic survival strategy. Apparently there are many examples in the arena of agriculture, particularly where "efficient" agronomic practices overrun the delicate interwoven tolerances of indigenous agriculture. Ecologists have a word for this type of agricultural efficiency: they call it "monocropping." By reducing the number of varieties in, say, a potato patch or a wheat field, the monocropping approach guarantees a much greater yield in the short

run. But, in the long run, it depletes the soil, diminishes the variety in
the system, and threatens the health and life of the plants and animals
living there.

Corporate systems that aim at maximizing short-term proceeds,
and disturb or cut out activities that operate in the margin of the company's "field," represent the business equivalent of monocropping. In
the long run, the parable of the Chilean potato suggests that these companies have greatly diminished chances of survival.

In retrospect, this comment from the Shell report seemed to resonate particularly closely with the parable of the Chilean potato:

> Successful companies tended to perceive other [internal] re-
> sources as being capable of development *in addition* to the ex-
> isting resource rather than *instead of*. . . . Many successful
> moves were made when companies did not see themselves
> locked into a particular business, but *in business,* with talents
> and resources that could be used profitably to meet a variety
> of consumer needs. Successful moves were relatively free of im-
> mediate pressure.[3]

Successful companies, in short, were free to go against the grain because
they had been cultivating, within themselves, a wide variety of potential activities.

## Tolerance and the Ecology of Companies

The choice between tolerance and intolerance, in the end, is a matter
of ecology. The choice depends in part on the organization's interrelationship with the other living beings in its world, and also on the organization's relationship with the living beings—including other organizations—within itself. By maintaining a certain level of variety within
itself, the living company is far more adaptable, because it is far more
capable of responding effectively to the variety of forces that exist in its
environment.

Intolerant companies can have long and healthy lives, provided that they have an appreciable amount of control over the world in which they live. The banking and insurance industries in many European countries lived for long times in this sort of world. So do many "postal, telephone, and telegraph" (PTT) companies, as long as their telecommunications bailiwicks are strongly regulated. Under monopolistic conditions, a stable market or other conditions in which the company maintains control, the managers will do well to optimize efficiency. They will go for maximum results with minimum resources. This minimization of resources inside the company requires an intolerant management style. There cannot be much room for delegated authority and freedom of action.

Instead of growing potatoes in an open environment like the Andes, these intolerant companies are growing potatoes in a glass house. In a glass house, the horticulturist controls the amount of heat, light, fertilizer, and humidity in the environment 24 hours a day. Over time, like the horticulturist, managers of intolerant companies become more and more clever at finding the optimum, most efficient methods for growing the potatoes in a controlled environment. There is a great deal of "learning by assimilation"—Piaget's term for taking in new information without changing one's fundamental way of thinking or acting. The managers' structures and knowledge base get honed over time to deal with a familiar world, but there is little learning by accommodation (making internal changes to fit a changing world).

The company will undeniably thrive for as long as the world remains stable. High tolerance, after all, is wasteful of resources. That is why a company with a lot of control over its environment has few reasons to be open or tolerant. Such a company may be lucky and live all its life in a world with a stable market for its products or services.

When the environment becomes unstable, however, there is a need for fast learning. Now, suddenly, the glass house cracks. The external environment, with all its unpredictabilities, reasserts itself. The managers must return to growing potatoes in the Andes. Diversity and openness are much better management dictums in those conditions, as the sample companies in the Shell study of corporate survivors demonstrate.

## Balancing Freedom and Control

Why, then, is it so difficult to switch from corporate monoculture to diversity? Why do managers resist the shift, even when they are keenly aware of the benefits that a practice of tolerance might bring?

Some might argue that monoculture remains compelling for managers because it continues to produce immediate results. Even if managers know those results stem from a temporary efficiency, at the expense of long-term survival they will hang onto the rewards they receive for bringing in "good numbers." But let's beware of easy criticism. As I said in the last chapter, in a crisis, the natural reaction is to centralize, to decide quickly, and to impose solutions.

Therefore, I think that there is more: the deeper reason why managers resist the notion of tolerance is the dilemma between the need to control, a need we discussed in Chapter 7, "Flocking," and the need for tolerance and freedom. These two needs, both equally desirable, are at first glance mutually exclusive. Freedom and tolerance are necessary to increase the learning abilities of the organization. Yet control is necessary to maintain its cohesion.

When push comes to shove, most managers will choose control. In fact, it is emotionally difficult, in most companies, even to *relax* the emphasis on control. Managers who are doers, accustomed to getting things done, will tend to trust themselves more than anybody else. They feel an emotional pull toward exercising power and domination, and they fear the chaos and uncertainty that come with letting go of the reins. If we let people have freedom, they'll simply "do anything they want," and the results will suffer.

And yet, the more changing and uncontrollable the world, the more evident become the dangers of control. Relying on a management policy of high internal and external controls puts a tremendous burden on the few "thinking" managers at the top. The capacity to make decisions becomes severely limited, and everything waits on the judgment of the few "trusted" people. By definition, the neck of a bottle is always in the top! This very basic dilemma is often couched in terms of the juxtaposition "to centralize or to decentralize?" Nowadays, almost everybody is in favor of decentralization, but few dare to risk the accompanying loss of control. That is why rational debates about centralization versus decentralization are seldom followed by rational decisions. Instead, managers tend to make kneejerk decisions, in which they abruptly move toward freedom and then suddenly retract back toward control, oscillating continually in one direction or the other.

For all these reasons, creating space—increasing the mobilization of internally available brain capacity—is always a tricky business. The dilemma between tolerance and control can only be solved, of course, by finding a way to meet *both* goals. Space must be created for people to experiment and take risks. At the same time, people cannot simply do "anything they like" at the expense of the organization's common purpose. Clearly, one needs both: empowered people and effective control.

## The Management of Tolerance

If you are a manager, to control can mean to keep down the cost per unit of output. On the contrary, a management that empowers is trying to increase the output per unit of costs. Good management knows that it will have to do both. Whether it aims simultaneously at both targets, or whether it will "wave" (oscillate) over time from more control to more tolerance and back,[4] an "either-or" attitude—opting for either control or tolerance—could be fatal in the long run.

Pursuing two contradictory goals is not easy. It should therefore not surprise us that, between the horns of this particular dilemma, a pseudosolution has sprung up over time. It is called "strategic planning." It sounds quite neat: if you have a strategy that tells you where you are going, you don't need to worry too much about loss of control. You can let people get on with their jobs, giving them freedom and space, because management supposedly has control over the company's direction and destination.

Disappointments with strategic planning were not slow in coming. As Henry Mintzberg describes in his history, *The Rise and Fall of Strategic Planning*, complaints and carps about strategic planning began to appear around 1973, and the criticism gathered momentum through the 1970s and 1980s. Moreover, strategic planning advocates could point to few successes. Even strategic planning in the military became discredited, as Robert S. McNamara's Planning-Programming-Budgeting System (PPBS) was blamed in part for the failures of the Vietnam War effort.[5]

The fact is that the word *strategy* tends to be misused. It should not be a noun; you should not "have" a strategy, in the sense of a document the organization follows. Rather, *strategy* should be a verb: strategy is something you *do,* rather than something you *have.*

One thing management can *do* in a company is *steer.* This is a very popular concept, both in management literature and among managers. In this concept, strategy (or "steering") is the art of management. It consists of the daily activity of steering the institution in a direction that will ensure that it, and the entities within it, move toward their full development. Henry Mintzberg noticed this himself in 1973; in his book *The Nature of Managerial Work,* he reported that managers, whom he had observed on the job, rarely sat back to plan in any abstract, cerebral sense. Instead, "strategies" emerged out of the give and take of day-by-day management activity.[6]

So let us talk, then, about the art of strategy and steering in a company that supposedly balances tolerance and control. When one thinks of steering, the metaphor of a ship comes to mind easily. Many a chairman, in his public statements, talks about "weathering the storm" or "changing tack" and "setting the course." The metaphor seems, at first glance, to fit well. In a company, as on a ship, there is a defined command structure with everyone in some sort of specialized activity. Some people run the machine room, some lift the anchor and hoist the sails. The boss, known as the "captain," exercises the necessary degree of control and discipline to ensure that the ship and crew act in unison. It is clear that the skipper is boss.

In this metaphor, the "ship" (or the company) is an asset manned by people. It sails from destination to destination to make profits for the owners. It has no interest in its own longevity. On a real ship, it would be inadmissible for the first mate or the boatswain to have the freedom to change to another tack or set another course. Chaos and anarchy would result; the ship could well run onto the cliffs. Of course, the skipper might sit down with the first mate and discuss the destination and how best to get there. He may even have a word with the helmsman. Yet the skipper carries the ultimate responsibility. Even so, the skipper knows that he is on this voyage only because another human voice has decided to send the ship to this destination. That voice is the owner's.

A living company, by contrast, is a living being. It moves from birth to death, seeking to extend its own potential. *There is no one steering.* Instead, the living company takes one step at a time. Each decision is followed by an action, and then new observations about the effect of that action, and then another step tomorrow. Before taking each new step, the company looks up and decides where to put its foot in the light of the conditions of the moment. There are no admiralty charts and no final destination, except death.

Such a company knows that it is capable of only certain accomplishments at this moment in its history. These capabilities restrict the number of places where it can put its foot today. It may also have some untapped potential for future actions. Developing that potential will increase the number of places where it can step tomorrow.

*In what direction are we steering?* Where do you steer a company like that without dissolving into anarchy? If you are a manager, the poet Machado has a quote for you which you might find relevant.

Life is a path that you beat while you walk it.[7]

To me, this line embodies the most profound lesson on planning and strategy that I have ever learned. When you look back, you see a clear path that brought you here. But you created that path yourself. Ahead, there is only uncharted wilderness.

You do not navigate a company to a predefined destination. You take steps, one at a time, into an unknowable future. There are no paths, no roads ahead of us. In the final analysis, it is the walking that beats the path. It is not the path that makes the walk.

*Who is doing the steering?* In 1994, an article in the *Financial Times* described how Britain's fifth largest building society, a savings and loan institution, had remained without a chief executive for 18 months. The lack of a CEO, noted some outside bankers and financial analysts, could affect the society's credit ratings. Yet, continued the article, "The existing management has acquired a better-than-adequate track record."[8]

The society had been run all that time by its finance director, its commercial director, and its information systems manager. This triumvirate worked closely with a ten-person management committee and a chairman who was available two days a week. Acting without a clear central power center, this banking institution increased its profits in 1993 by 22 percent and in the first quarter of 1994 by 37 percent. Remarked the *Financial Times:* "The longer this has continued, the more Leeds executives may question what even a paragon [CEO] will bring to the organization."[9] Only one doubt, in fact, remained: "Competitors accept that [the triumvirate] has done a competent job and have the backing of Leeds' staff, but there remains a question about strategic issues."[10]

Think carefully about this latter concern. Why should there be a problem about strategy? It was clear the organization had one, and an ever-evolving one at that. Otherwise, it could not have made decisions for a year and a half. In other words, in this company a CEO was not necessary to elaborate a strategy.

But one might have had an immediate negative effect. An incoming chief executive, who would likely come from the outside, would probably take a thoroughly different view of the way forward. He could use his position of power to make a U-turn away from a demonstrably profitable policy. All he would achieve would be to create uncertainty in an otherwise well-performing organization.

The moral of this story is clear. A company does not unconditionally need a single hand at the tiller. The personal use of power to steer does not necessarily serve a healthy purpose. It could reduce the number of brains engaged in the "planning-as-learning" activity, and it could be seriously disorienting.

Many companies are similar to this savings and loan institution. To be sure, there may be a CEO who espouses strategy and sets policy. But the real decision making occurs in a diffused, tolerant, "planning-as-learning" environment.

*Setting of the context as an alternative to steering.* In all but the smallest of companies and in all situations but a crisis, it would be wise to be careful with an action-oriented management style. This does not mean that we do away with all leadership and hierarchy. Management plays an indispensable role, but it is not in the first place one of looking out of the bridge window, setting the course on the compass, and opening the throttle.

It is the company as a whole that beats Machado's path while it walks. The company as a whole should scan the environment, decide on the next step, determine where to set a foot, and when to do so. To engage as many brains as available and possible in this process is a complicated matter.

The art of managing—of coaching such a community along its path—becomes a matter of setting the context for the rest of the organization's members to perform that task at their level.

This cycle of seeing, concluding, deciding, and acting is, of course, the cycle of continuous learning described in Chapter 4, "Decision Making as a Learning Activity." In this sense, strategy is simply the development of the organization's ability to learn. The organization's ability to learn faster (and possibly better) than the competition becomes its most sustainable competitive advantage.

Senior management must set the context and the process within which the maximum of the organization's available brain capacity engages in continuous learning. The design and the running of these processes is a line management responsibility which cannot be delegated. Rachel Bodle, reporting on a series of workshops on change management, describes the demands on leadership that occur in a turbulent world. The new forms of leadership, she writes, involved

> demonstrating willingness to "let go" in a new, open, more informal and less hierarchical style of management; allocating time to get wide recognition and acceptance of the need for change; encouraging risk taking by ensuring that mistakes are not penalized if there is learning; dispensing with authority and suspending with hierarchy so that learning can take place; providing necessary feedback; [and] creating an environment for teamwork.[11]

Management can be helped by planners in this effort. If management is a learning process, then planners can be helpers or enablers in the learning process—and no more than that. Learning starts with perception. Planners can encourage the company to look up more often and to look further ahead. They can help make the learning process more deliberate and make sure that more of the available brainpower is engaged. They can develop methods for making sure that individual inventiveness becomes shared knowledge before the next corporate foot is put forward.

So, if strategy is something you *do,* I have little doubt in my mind that this doing actually constitutes learning, not steering. This embodiment of learning within the strategic process, in the end, also determines the organizational role of the scenario work that we examined in Chapter 3, "Tools for Foresight." Scenarios institutionalize a process of learning (and exchange of learning) throughout the company. With that in place, the company can afford to tolerate its diversity of marginal activities, because the act of learning keeps the company cohesive, without the need for strict regulation by authority.

# 9

# The Corporate Immune System

NO MATTER HOW VITAL TOLERANCE MAY BE FOR A LIVING COM-
pany, there are dangers in tolerance and openness. These are not the
dangers that most managers associate with tolerance. They have nothing to do with loss of internal control, or with inefficiency. Like human
beings, corporations have immune systems, and when the corporate immune system cannot cope with the openness of a tolerant company, the
resulting stress puts the entire organization in danger.

In the human body, the immune system is built into the cells within
the bloodstream. Its role is to maintain an equilibrium with the intruders from the outside world that continuously enter the body. The
active cells of the immune system can detect these outside organisms
and, if necessary, secrete chemicals to defend the body against them.
The more capable the immune system, the more resistant the host body
is to harmful effects from bacteria, viruses, fungi, or parasites. These
intruders from the outside are not prevented from entering, nor are they
systematically destroyed on every incursion. The immune system keeps
them in check while they exist within the body.

Francisco Varela describes the functioning of the immune system
in this manner: if you take an airplane, for example, from New York

City to Rio de Janeiro, you move your body between two very different molecular soups—two environments of completely different bacteria, fungi, and viruses. When you get off the plane in Rio, your immune
system begins to "recruit" new cells from the regular flow of lympho-
cytes that your body produces in the spinal column and releases into
the bloodstream. Some of these potential antibody cells will be called
into action, depending on the new molecular environment in which you
wade.

Each day, your immune system recruits enough new cells to con-
stitute up to 20 percent of its own population. Your body, during that
recruitment process, rebuilds an equilibrium with the unfamiliar intruders of the Rio atmosphere. This makes the human immune system,
according to Varela, into an extremely open system—and thus a good
learning system.[1]

Unfortunately, there are limits to the number of intrusions that the
human body can handle. The tolerance of any body has an upper value.
Thus imagine that you are put into an environment in which more than
25 percent of the invaders consist of a new type. Or suppose you are
invaded by a particularly virulent organism. In that case, the intruder
from the outside is numerous or powerful enough to exceed your immune system's capacity to learn.

Now you have an infection. Instead of learning and incorporating
the new molecules, the immune system must repel. It increases the body
temperature to make life more difficult for the new intruders, and it develops a composition of antibodies and killer cells to cope with new
types of intruders.

Without thinking, your body has moved into a mode of resistance
and rejection. This is not necessarily beneficial for you. You experience
a fever, exhaustion, headaches, and tension in your digestive system.
The reaction to the entrance of a foreign substance may even have more
severe effects. Your resistance and rejection may upset your own equilibrium so much that it could lead to shock or even death.

This state of affairs is as true for corporations as it is for individuals. The health of a company is under constant attack from the inside
and the outside. The attacks come from individuals or groups of individuals who do not want to be part of the whole. They are there for

their own purposes. It does not matter how honorable or dishonorable these purposes may be. The health of the community is under threat.

On the inside, the threats may come from groups of individuals who are not full members of the community. (They may see themselves that way, or they may have been deliberately cast as nonmembers at the time of recruitment.) They are insiders and intimately familiar with the company. They are the "hands" that operate the machines. But they are not part of "us."

Recently, these internal "nonmembers" have grown in number. During exercises of staff reductions and downsizing, many people who had thought themselves members have been told of a sudden alteration in their status. They may still be needed for capacity reasons or because the laws made outright dismissal difficult and time consuming. But they have been told, explicitly or implicitly, that they should no longer see their future as aligned with that of the company.

We should not be surprised to discover that these internal non-members will often feel detached from the company or angry with it. Many will feel the need to affiliate into another institutional body such as a trade union, if only to defend themselves. If that happens, there are then two institutional bodies, a company and a trade union, cohabiting the same space with very different goals. This will inevitably have some impact on the corporate health; possibly benevolent, possibly malevolent, depending on whether these two personae will elect for a symbiotic or an inimical coexistence.

When a company tells some of its members that they are no longer "us," the company also defines a new group: "who is left of us." If that definition is made very narrow, the company may find that it has few real members left with loyalty to the whole. In some cases, too few members are left. Those who still fall under the definition of "us" should understand beyond doubt that they are part of the whole. The company should make it doubly clear to them that the development of their full potential is still reasonably assured by holding together in a symbiotic relationship.

Other threats to the health of the company come from outside. These might include customers with a different set of expectations; new teams of decision makers from a merger or acquisition; or key members of the corporate community who just don't seem to "fit right" with the prevailing ethos.

Just like the human body, the corporate body needs an immune system which can treat different types of intruders appropriately. For one thing, just as with the human body, the vast majority of intruders are beneficial. Humans are constantly invaded by bacteria and viruses whose impact is symbiotic with our own health and survival. The same is true of companies; most invaders bring with them new perspectives and capabilities. Moreover, even if we wanted to, we could not keep intruders out of either a human body or a corporation; they cannot be kept out of an open system. Openness inevitably means that something other than oneself enters one's body.

But you can react to these intruders discriminatingly. Some may indeed have to be repelled, even at the cost of upsetting the company's equilibrium. Some should be managed, so that their encroachment comes gradually enough to let the immune system build up a response. And some should be embraced as necessary vehicles for the organization's learning.

## Acquisitions and Mergers

Consider, for example, the case of acquisitions and mergers. These represent one of the irresistible temptations to which managers of "economic companies" are subjected. Acquisitions and mergers carry the double promise of "buying knowledge off the shelf" (gaining capabilities without having to go through a change or conduct any learning yourself) and making the company bigger (and thereby, one hopes, stronger) in an adversarial world.

But ask people who have lived through an acquisition or a merger about the experience during the first few years. It is not unlike the first three or four days after catching the flu. The temperature of the institution is quite high; it is as if there is a "fever" in the air. There are headaches; people feel an uncanny, unpredicted exhaustion. And there may be a sense that the larger company can't quite "digest" the smaller one. In fact, all sorts of rejection mechanisms are in place. Most notably, during the first four or five years after a merger and acquisition, there is an enormous shift of individuals entering and exiting the affected units. The institution is mobilizing its immune system—and rejecting a great deal of the incoming culture.

In biological terms, a merger or an acquisition represents an intrusion of foreign bodies, ideas, and values into the host organization. If you acquire a competitor who is 25 percent of your size, you have accepted an intrusion of 25 percent of your existing population. A 50-50 merger with a foreign partner means an intrusion of 50 percent for each of the two partners.

At these proportions, many acquisitions and most mergers are likely to rise well above the tolerance limits of both partners. Acquisitions and mergers are *infections*. That is why the temperature goes up and the corporate body goes into a resistance mode. Many cases of this resistance have been well documented. Management professor Michael Porter analyzed 2,700 mergers and acquisitions by 33 major U.S. companies over a 36-year period (1950 to 1986); his report, published in 1987, found failure rates between 50 and 75 percent ("failure" meaning "disposal"). A Dutch study in the prestigious journal *Economisch-Statistische Berichten* found failure rates of up to 60 percent in similar situations.[2]

Moreover, many managers carry the scars of their own personal experience. After a merger, two internal tribes look at each other in distrust, personnel policies remain affected by premerger values for a long time after the original intrusion, and staff will feel deep levels of distrust and suspicion about every major personnel move.

I am well acquainted with a number of people who were involved in the merger of two banks in the Netherlands. This merger took place 20 years ago, and the people I know are now 60 years old or older. Yet they can still remember vividly which of the premerger employees worked for the other bank. To them, the other bank *still* represents an infection that was never fully assimilated.

The tribes within the merged institution continue to see themselves as separate entities. If I come to your country as part of the merger of our companies, you will still see me as an outsider. You will trust me less than someone from your home institution. On the next promotion you make, you will seek out someone from your own bank; and on my part, I will attribute my failure to get the job to the fact that you are a member of the other tribe. Thus we will trust each other even less as time goes on.

Royal Dutch/Shell experienced this problem for 50 years. It was formed through the merger of two parent companies: The Royal Dutch oil company, and the British firm Shell Transport and Trading. They merged in 1907; but when I joined in 1951, the two parent companies still had quite separate organizations based in the Hague and London, respectively. It was as if two single parents had come together in marriage, putting all their children together into one household, but sleeping in separate bedrooms. The marriage was not consummated until a series of personnel policies introduced in the mid-1950s began to integrate the worldwide Shell community, followed by a McKinsey reorganization which finally created one integrated organization spread over the two central offices.

Another Shell example dates from the period in the early 1970s when "diversification" was fashionable. Royal Dutch/Shell bought a medium-sized metal company, Billiton. In terms of people, capitalization, turnover, or any other measurement, the Shell Group was so much bigger than Billiton that Shell could absorb this acquisition without any difficulty. However, by any standard, Shell's intrusion was way above Billiton's tolerance level.

Shell did not show a rejection mechanism. But Billiton did. The Billiton entity ailed and, in effect, died. Less than a decade later, nearly all of the senior Billiton managers had left—notwithstanding the utmost care Shell had exerted to leave the original Billiton management in control. We had tried to prevent Shell managers from overpowering the new family member, but the ecological relationship between the two companies made that impossible. For Billiton, the merger represented an infection and had to be repelled. This meant that Shell was unable to reap the benefits that we had hoped might emerge from the Billiton measure. Shell was simply too big for Billiton.

There is no easy way to manage mergers and acquisitions, once the bankers have left. The infection analogy is useful, in my mind, because it shows why money cannot buy intelligence, knowledge, and innovative new behavior in large quantities. Learning is not a matter of "filling up the tank" by buying a new partnership. Learning is a process.

Partnership takes time. And if one partner has too much power to interfere, whether it intends to interfere or not, then the merger and acquisition process will, in itself, set off resistance mechanisms that defeat the original purpose that brought the merger into being in the first place.

## Parasites

The less a company operates in control of its environment, the more open it should be: foreign bodies and ideas will be able to enter easily. That is as it should be; indeed, it becomes a strength of the company. However, the company can never be sure how these bodies and ideas will behave, once inside. Every intruder has a choice: it can select a symbiotic relationship or it can pursue its own benefit, to the exclusion of all others.

All intruders are not alike. Richard Dawkins, who has written at length about the role of intruders and parasites in evolution, describes them all as egoistic. None of them "cares" about the welfare of the host body, except as a vehicle for their own survival. They serve their own genetic interests. At the same time, however, many of them serve the host body well: They are symbiotic, increasing the sophistication and capability of the host body at the same time that they remain dedicated to their own interests. There are bacteria that live in beetles, for example, and use the beetles' eggs as transport into the bodies of new beetles. They do not obstruct the reproductive process of the beetle; indeed, they depend on it.[3]

Others are parasitic: they bring lasting damage to the host body. Dawkins offers a fascinating explanation of the difference between a symbiotic intruder and a parasite. The parasite *plans its exit on its own terms*. Any other intruder exits through the host's natural functions and systems, such as excretion and procreation. A parasite breaks through the host's natural functions, exiting in a way that may destroy or harm the host.

Dawkins gives the example of a snail that is infested by a parasite (a fluke of the genus *Leucochloridium*) that burrows into its tentacles and causes them to swell. Those swelling tentacles (which happen to contain eyes), in turn, protrude more obviously and look like "tempting morsels" to a particular type of bird. In this way, the snail becomes more susceptible to being caught by that bird. And the fluke now gains a larger host body, the bird, to enter. This is part of the life cycle of that particular parasite.

If you see a snail with a protruding eye, and you want to know why that eye evolved, you should not necessarily ask, "Why is a protruding eye in the interest of that snail?" Instead, says Dawkins, you ask, "Whose interest is served by the protrusion of this eye?"

And that question will lead you to the parasite.

Destructive parasites can also exist anywhere in the corporate host body. They can be excluded individuals or even individuals in positions of power, but planning their exit on their own terms. Power can be used to manipulate the definition of "us" in the service of someone else's strategy. A senior manager manipulating a situation to make his or her own résumé look good, but leaving all the rest vulnerable, is behaving parasitically. Similarly, when a division of a company resents being part of the whole, that division can easily become a parasite in the host body. It does not matter whether this resentment is justified. (For instance, when the added value of the company's head office is less than the costs the host office imposes on a resentful outpost, that outpost is *still* a destructive parasite.)[4] All of these people and subsystems, in Richard Dawkins's sense, are serving their own self-interest at the expense of the natural functions of the host company.

If a company begins to perform seemingly self-destructive acts, you should not ask, "Why is this activity in the interest of the corporation?" You should ask, "Whose interest is served by this self-destructive act?" Is it the small group that has misused its power to define the company as only the five or six top people? Is it the large intestinal snail called a partner company, a division, or a trade union?

This biological view does not distinguish between inherently good or bad behavior—even if it were possible to define what is good or bad. Consider, for instance, a highly intolerant institution, which hires a group of consultants to improve its practices. Now, new ideas and new people enter the firm, with the intention of opening up the institution's behavior and improving its chances of survival. This intent is assuredly "good"—but to the existing (intolerant) membership, the intruders' behavior will seem "bad" and parasitic. The corporate immune system will go into action. The temperature will go up, and killer cells may finish off the intruding ideas. When this happens, it should not be taken as a comment on the quality of those ideas. It is a reaction to the strength of the host system's immunity mechanisms.

## Corporate Symbiosis

We normally think of intruders as parasites and of parasites as entering with the intention of weakening their hosts. This need not always be the case. On entry, every intruder has the same choice: a symbiotic relationship or a parasitic one. Indeed, there is a great deal of leverage available from cultivating symbiotic relationships with organizational parasites. To understand such relationships, the critical question is this: Why would certain people or substructures work with a kind of group loyalty to one another when others would not?

Dawkins answers this question as Stern did before him: All the members that stand to gain from tying their fate to the host institution will "cooperate." They will work together to make the whole institution behave as a single coherently purposeful unit. The primary difference between members and parasites, then, will have to do with their method of exit. Members will retire, whereas parasites will serve for their own sweet time and leave by a different route.

Under those conditions, it is clear that management's responsibility for guarding the corporate health is best served by preventive medicine and setting a context for mutual cooperation. Make sure, when a new member enters, that there is a shared value system in place. When a new member enters the system, make sure that there is a contract based on long-term harmonization of goals, as we discussed in Chapter 6, "Managing for Profit or for Longevity," under "Joining the Flow."

In this way, the company has the highest certainty that entrants will elect for member status, instead of becoming parasites. Money is not enough of an incentive. If the salary and bonus levels represent the sole or the most important condition of the contract between company and individual, the chances are increased that the lure of larger amounts of money will lead to parasitic behavior. This will be even more true for people who are in a closer position to higher amounts of money. The management levels in a company are the most propitious, from a parasite's point of view!

Money, in fact, needs a lot of attention in a living company. As every businessperson knows, money has as many attractions as it has roles to play within a company. It is the means by which the company gets access to resources—by which it remunerates its people and its shareholders. It can be the life blood that attracts predators and parasites, but it also plays an important role in the evolution of a company over its lifetime. Let us, therefore, turn our attention there next.

# EVOLUTION

# 10

# Conservatism in Financing

IN THE PART OF THIS BOOK ON ECOLOGY, I MADE THE CASE THAT openness and learning create the necessary *conditions* for a company's longevity and survival. Openness improves learning; without an effective learning capability, a company cannot hope to "evolve" effectively in an unpredictable world. Evolution is the process of a company's development, and managers who are attuned to this can influence the *speed* and the *means* (the "how") of the evolution they set in motion.

Intuitively, we can see that money must play an important role in a company's survival and evolution. With money, a company can buy resources (and time), which allow it to evolve more rapidly. In addition, people who see companies as machines for earning money measure the success of a company's evolution by the extent to which it can make more money than its competitors.

Equally, the success of entrepreneurs (those particularly successful participants in the corporate game) is generally measured in terms of the amounts of money they can produce—either in the size of their business' revenues or in the amount they can return to the company's owners.

If the amount of money is the primary measure of corporate success, then it is obvious that any company could never have enough cash
coming in. But is that the only function money serves? Could it also
take part in governing the evolution of a company? Could it be that
having too much money could lead to a quick or unbalanced growth
and development? Or, that leaving too little money in the company by
siphoning off too much for individual members (or parasites) could reduce the survival chances of that company?

Many people will immediately agree with the latter statement: an
unbalanced distribution of money could well threaten the future via-
bility of the company. But how easy that can be done and what form it
would take is illustrated by a talk that Dick Onians, a managing partner of the Baring Venture fund, gave at the Royal Society of Arts in London in 1994. Barings, he said, had invested in about 200 company startups during the previous decade. But only 40 of them had developed into
profitable and sustainable businesses. Of the remaining 160 companies,
20 percent had failed outright. The other 120 companies, he said, faced
three probable destinies: "to be acquired by a larger company; to merge
with competitors; or to regress to being life-style businesses for a small
group of owner-managers."[1]

In short, although they might survive, they would not sustain
themselves as the sort of entities that had been foreseen for them. To
understand the high mortality rate of these newborn startups, and to
discover the factors behind the few successes, Mr. Onians conducted a
review of ten successful startups and ten failures. Marketing, strategic
positioning, and product development, he found, were important; but
they were subsidiary to another set of factors. The companies' survival
rose or fell on the way they managed their resources: their people, their
information, and their money.

In earlier chapters, we have looked at the way companies manage
their information (in the part on Learning) and their people (in Persona
and Ecology). But the nature of money is particularly misunderstood.
Every living entity consumes; and money serves, in a large corporation,
as the way of measuring what has been consumed. As a result of this
role, when properly managed, the financing of a company becomes the
governor on a living company's growth and evolution.

In this case, I do not use the word *governor* in its purely political sense, to imply a state leader or authoritarian director. The financing of a company is a governor in the sense of a regulator—like the valve on a furnace, which adjusts the flow of fuel and thereby indirectly controls the production of heat.

For the startup businesses that Mister Onians studied, financing would act as a governor by regulating the incoming flow of cash and thereby indirectly modulating the growth of the company. Apart from its own cash generation, there were only three ways that further financing could become available. The company could borrow. It could accept equity capital in return for shares. Or it could engineer a hybrid of the other two methods.

Borrowing to finance the startup was an almost irresistible temptation. For, as Mister Onians put it, that would allow the founders to maintain control of the firm.

> By working with borrowed money, management can retain a larger share of the equity—indeed, ideally keep 100%. Thus, by remaining the dominant owners, management can award themselves salaries, perquisites, bonuses, pensions, and eventually, dividends with no deference to other shareholders or their board representatives.[2]

This may seem a sensible way to build a business: get the bank to cough up the money, pay it its due in the form of interest, and keep all the value accumulation to the inner circle of founders and the initiators. At the same time, with borrowed money, there is a much wider limit to what a company can accomplish in its early years.

But consider the results, as Mister Onians and his colleagues found them in practice:

> Entrepreneurs [with] high debt, high expense, [and] low equity under perform entrepreneurs who go for high dependence on share owners' funds. Nine out of the ten failing businesses were highly dependent on short term debt. In five of these cases it was their so-called "friends," the bankers, who pulled the rug from under them and dictated . . . the terms and conditions for the demise of their businesses.[3]

The picture was very different in the ten successful companies, all of which eventually became significant international businesses. Eight out of the ten had never held a loan. They were entirely debt free and always had been. The two companies that had borrowed money had done so to meet specific short-term needs. They had since repaid the debts in full.

Conservatism in financing, in short, is not merely a conceit of a former, less credit-happy age. It seems to be an essential condition for companies that hope to survive to a ripe old age. When companies know how to "listen" to their financing, they are ready to follow the path of a natural, long-lived evolution.

## Money as the Governor of Evolution

At Shell, we had found something similar in our report on long-lived corporations. Nearly every company over the average age had a conservative approach to its financing. If not debt free, then they were rigidly careful about their borrowing and investment capital. In short, they knew the value of having money in the kitty.

At first, it may seem paradoxical to limit the speed of a company's growth by its capacity to generate its own funds. In its growth stages, any company that is willing to borrow can theoretically operate without constraints. Such a company has the options that stem from not having to rely on its own money reserves or the equity it can raise from investors. This makes revolutionary change possible, to be sure; the results are more instantly dramatic, and the change may indeed be more effective.

But growth through borrowing money, or through mergers and acquisitions, is dangerous precisely *because* it is not constrained. At some point, the pendulum will shift. Having to service your debt, you lose the options that come from having "spare cash in the kitty." You can no longer choose your moment.

Long-lived companies know that having money in hand means that they have flexibility and independence of action, when competitors do not. Having built up their business organically, they can grasp opportunities without having to convince third-party financiers of the attractiveness of their decisions. They can even make business decisions without having to depend on purely financial considerations. Money in hand has made them masters of their own timing.

In this way, conservatism in financing serves as a governor to keep the speed of your company's evolution at an appropriate scale. That does not necessarily mean a small scale. James Collins and Jerry Porras report that Hewlett-Packard managers eschewed long-term debt, a seemingly irrational policy. But,

> by refusing to take on long-term debt in order to fund growth, HP forced itself to learn how to fund its 20-plus percent average annual growth . . . entirely from within. Such a mechanism . . . produced a whole company of incredibly disciplined general managers operating with a level of leanness and efficiency usually only found in small, cash-constrained companies.[4]

To follow the model of evolution, a conservative finance policy helps a great deal, and may even be necessary. A businessperson's life is full of irresistible temptations, and the most irresistible of all is probably impatience. We often get into positions in which we have the power to foster quick growth, with impressive short-term results—at the expense of the long-term health of the enterprise. If there are negative consequences to this growth, the consequences won't be felt for months or years. So, instead of evolution, we go for revolution. Instead of building an enterprise, we set out on a quick adventure. We take a gamble.

But good businesspeople are not gamblers. They should be the opposite; they are stewards and custodians of the company they manage. Conservatism in financing helps them avoid the temptation of gambling.

Whenever I mention this point in speeches, I immediately see roughly half the audience nodding in agreement. Those of us who have managed the pursestrings of an organization know full well how virtuous conservatism in financing can be. Why, then, do many managers have such difficulty putting it into practice? I believe that the difficulty begins with our definition of corporate success.

## Money as the Measure of Corporate Success

In an "economic company," one that sees itself as existing primarily to maximize profits and assets, the criterion for success is clear. The larger you grow, the more assets you can command. The less resources you use in the process, the more profits you can deliver. In this way, the dominant school of thought on business administration measures success purely in terms of quantity: the *maximization* of revenues, market share, share value, or proceeds. A place in the Financial Times 100 or the Fortune 500 is the symbol of such success, and you only reach that position by growing larger.

These criteria belong to the concept of a company as a money-making machine. Managing moneymaking machines is reassuring and comforting. It makes the company feel rational, calculable, and controllable. The economic company is thus a counterpart to the *Homo economicus* of my business school professors in the 1950s: a perfectly rational creature, making choices based on self-interest—and entirely unrelated to anything in real life.

But a healthy company does not measure its success in terms of money or profits. In the research conducted by Collins and Porras, for example, there was no indication that success factors included such economic measures of success as low-cost marketing, being at the cutting edge of technology, or being a high value-added producer. "Existing first and foremost to maximize profits" was even specifically relegated to a much lower priority![5]

Ten years earlier, the researchers of the Shell longevity study had used soft, noneconomic words to describe the successful long-surviving companies. These companies were "financially conservative," we wrote, "with a staff which identifies with the company and a management which is tolerant and sensitive to the world in which they live."

William Stern had written, 70 years earlier, that the basic driving force of every living system is the development of its inherent potential. The long-lived companies we studied at Shell seemed to realize this force and to live up to its demands.

Everything *about* the company—its physical business, its assets, its policies and practices—was a means for living. None of these constituted the purpose of the company. Success for the company meant evolving into the best possible thing it could be and, in the process, to be good at what it happens to be doing in order to survive.

Shell's purpose is not to deliver oil, to produce energy, or even to better the material wealth and capability of industrial society. It has to be good at those activities to make the profits to achieve its primary purposes: to survive and to develop new potential as necessary in an evolving society. Shell does not "exist to pump oil." We pump oil in order to exist.

This view runs contrary to a lot of what is *said and written* about companies, by both insiders and outsiders. But it is very consistent with the way that companies act (independent of what they may say).

It is also very consistent with the way most managers' minds work when they think about the ultimate purpose of their company. When executives retreat for a weekend to formulate a corporate purpose in terms of a mission statement, they mount rapidly up a ladder of abstraction. The phrase, "British Gas is a company to distribute natural gas in Great Britain" is quickly replaced with "British Gas is a worldwide energy company."

Mission statements are often justifiably criticized because they don't seem to say anything, once all the abstractions are in place. But the *phenomenon* of this abstraction is worth noting; it is so consistent, from company to company, that it must exist for a reason. I believe the reason is that every businessperson knows, in his or her heart, that too narrow a definition of the business is literally life threatening. For long-term survival, a company cannot be defined in terms of the business which it happens to be doing at this very moment. Like the long-term surviving companies out of the Shell study, it may have to change its business portfolio several times over. In addition, to develop the options it needs for survival, it may have to go through periods in which return on investment to shareholders takes second place to reinvestment to further develop the company's long-term capabilities.

A long-term survivor, in short, does not define its life in economic terms, but in terms of its own evolution: the development of the entity as a whole, including all the people who have joined the contract with it, so that it and they are part of each other's identity.

To live with a sense of purpose so far removed from the economic definition of companies may be refreshing. For example, it may allow for patience. Evolution, in human living systems and in corporate systems, takes place over long periods of time. Paradoxically, however, this long, slow process allows relatively fast adaptation to a changing environment, creating conditions for the development of the organism's potential.

I do not argue that *all* companies should live according to this principle. Many companies, and their managers, have thrived by remaining economic companies, especially where they were in control of their external environment. However, I argue that managers must be acutely aware of *which* type of company they happen to be managing. To espouse the ideas of a living company while implementing the practices of an economic company could do great damage, because the management practices that fit one type of company are incompatible with the other. In the end, the choice between these two companies will come down, not to the rhetoric espoused by the executives, but to the way it manages its information, its people, and its finances.

It is in this light that we should look at the concept of corporate growth. In an economic company, growth is an unequivocal good. But a conservative financier is concerned about the *speed* and *quality* of growth. Will it contribute to the company's evolution, to its development to be the best that it can be, in fit with its environment? If not, then that growth will not be seen as successful.

## Money as the Expression of Corporate Reality

Just as most company manuals represent yesterday's writeup of the day before yesterday's solution to last year's problems, so the law tends to run similarly far behind reality. For example, there are distinct differences between the way banks behaved 50 years ago and the way they deal with corporate clients in distress today. But bankruptcy laws are based on these long-deceased banking practices of the previous half-century.

Worse still are the prevailing laws—and the social attitudes behind them—concerning the role of managers. Corporation laws in many

Western countries proclaim the investor, as the capital supplier and asset owner, to be the carrier of ultimate power: the power to decide the
life or death of a company. Managers are supposed to optimize capital
before all other concerns, or else they may be liable for damages.

But these laws, which give top priority to the rights of shareholders, are based on the assumption that the human elements are mere extensions of the capital assets. As a result, in concentrating our minds
on the optimization of the present capital asset base, we managers run
a serious risk of shortening the lifespan of our companies.

This is one of today's great dilemmas. And enlightened chief executives understand it very well. They recognize the value of community,
and of building trust. But they might break out of a conversation about
these values by saying that the next morning they have to address a
meeting of financial analysts, or confer with the corporate counsel. In
other words, they are caught between two imperatives: the external realities created by the law and the internal needs of managing with
knowledge as the most critical factor. Many CEOs cope by saying one
thing in public while they face a different reality inside the company.

## New Governance Forms in a Living Company

Shareholders are suppliers of capital in the same way that banks are
suppliers of money. They have a legally different position and get a
slightly different form of remuneration. Instead of interest payments,
they receive dividends, and they can sell their stock at a profit (or loss).
Although they are officially the "owners" of the company, their *func-
tional* role (from the company's point of view) is merely that of suppliers of money. They provide cash in return for equity.

To an economic company under today's legislation, that role as
suppliers of money is all that shareholders need to be considered as
owners. After all, an economic company exists in an environment
where capital is the most critical asset, and shareholders are the suppliers of that most critical asset.

Managers in an economic company know that their success depends on showing results—fast. And they get very little patience from

shareholders or other outsiders: the law or political regulators. They cannot talk freely in public about the need for reinvesting in the company to build up new, long-term potential or for building a cushion of cash to provide options for evolution. They find it difficult to say, "Look, we will have our ups and downs. But 10 or 20 years from now, you'll have the returns that would be far beyond anything you could extract from the company today."

Even if some shareholders were sympathetic, the company would be legally vulnerable. More seriously, it could throw itself open to an attempt by raiders to forcibly take over the firm. Many people who deal in investment aren't interested in long-term futures. They deal in present-day value. The discount factors in capital are so high that 20 years from now is practically worthless to the shareholder.

A living company, however, cannot have the same relationship with shareholders. To a living company, these suppliers of money are much like the other stakeholders in the external environment: unions, material suppliers, customers, shareholders, local government bodies, and the community around the plant. All of these are critically important forces within the outside environment. The company must remain in harmony with all of them. But they are not members. They are not part of the company's persona. It is not necessarily in the best interests of the company to obey them.

Yet, as critical parts of the company's external environment, the company should be engaged in constant conversation with them. Such dialogues are, unfortunately, rare in the current system. Conventionally, shareholders and managers do not converse. Even in a takeover, the new owner of 51 percent of the stock does not hold an in-depth conversation with the managers of the old regime. The new owner simply enters and dictates. The majority of shares conveys that legal power, and the persona of the living company cannot hold up against it. After all, the new dictator has not been a member of the old company. He has not entered the river at any point. He has not contributed or gained the trust of others in the enterprise. He has simply bought his way into the system. He will be an infection, and the old system will respond by resisting . . . or by dying.

Under those conditions, many senior managers turn river companies into economic companies. They are not willfully destructive. They are simply trying to do their best against the background of a terrible dilemma. When shareholders and outside regulatory bodies ask about the senior managers' results, they do not ask about efforts to improve community. They do not inquire about the company's prospects for a long and prosperous existence. They ask, "What is your return on capital employed?" "Aren't you overcapitalized?" and "What is your productivity?" In many cases, *because there is no communication with managers as members of a common entity,* the shareholders will apply any pressure they can to force fast return on assets at the expense of the company's long-term development.

To change this situation may be beyond the power of any single company. The shareholder-manager relationship may not express corporate reality very well, but it is embedded in the law. As such, the law is an anachronism. It is yesteryear's writeup of the situation before World War II, when capital was a scarce resource that deserved special protection and management attention to optimize its use.

In the intervening 50 years, capital has become much less scarce than it was before, even during the postwar years. In addition, the personalities of the suppliers of capital have changed. The link between the individual who makes the original saving and the commercial institution that finally obtains this saved capital to use in its wealth creation process has become far less direct than it was a half-century ago. Much shareholder power today is held by institutions such as large banks and pension funds, which pursue their own institutional interests. These interests can quite easily be detrimental to the company in which the shares are held.

The resulting tension between the business realities and the legal fiction of corporate ownership is evident for everybody to read in the daily newspapers. Some companies act according to the legal fiction and sacrifice thousands of people to safeguard assets or improve profitability. Others will focus on the business realities and scuttle hundreds of millions of dollars to keep themselves alive. In the choice between sacrificing assets or sacrificing people, business no longer gives automatic preference to the capital factor as the law allows or sometimes even demands. This is not because these managers have become more socially aware or people-conscious, but because it makes good business sense. A company that pulls through a crisis with its human talent mostly in place carries a real promise of a better outcome, both for its capital suppliers and for its people. Yet managers who act in accordance with this reality make themselves vulnerable to the law.

National legislation will begin to reflect the emerging reality of the new era only after these issues have crystallized in a public debate. That will take time, perhaps years. I write this with regret because, in the meanwhile, there is much room remaining for the abuse of the dominant legal powers given to the capital suppliers. Many more companies will be thrown wide open to parasitic and predatory behavior. This could, in fact, be a generic reason for the low average life expectancy of companies.

Many readers of this book will be shareholders themselves, and all of us are citizens. In both of these roles, we should be concerned about the price of corporate demise. The disappearance of a company is not gratuitous. A company's untimely mortality is hurtful and damaging to almost everyone concerned, including its shareholders.

## Why Not Let Corporations Die?

Some years ago, a Dutch television reporter asked me, after a speech I had given on the living company, "Why is it so important that Shell should survive?"

The question took me by surprise. To me it was so natural that companies should seek their own survival. I had seen nothing else in my life. Companies struggle to keep going and to grow, for as long as possible.

But the reporter was not asking about the company's intentions. He was questioning its value. What is so special about Shell, or any other company, that it should continue to clutter the earth with its presence? Why should it continue to exist when its utility for mankind would diminish or disappear?

The question takes on added relevance in an era when institutional shareholders and corporate raiders approve the buying of companies and dismantling them into component parts. We scrap a car at the end of its useful life. So, why not scrap a company?

It is a rightful question—if, indeed, the company is an economic company. Then it is a machine to produce a product, or to produce money and profits. And machines can be scrapped when their utility has ended.

But if it is a living company, then it is a persona, with a community of people embedded in it. And most people do not feel it is ethically correct to scrap a persona or a community.

All living beings have a right to exist. At the purely biological level, the question is not even asked. In nature, he who survives has earned the right to live.

Companies, as it happens, have a terrific internal will to live. We rarely hear of a company committing suicide. It can be done; all that would be required is liquidating the assets and giving the shares back to the shareholders. In liquidation, the solid body of the company is literally converted into fluid capital. I believe this deliberate act is far less frequent, per capita, than suicide among people.

It is hard to imagine that corporate suicide can be done with decency. Indeed, when the subject of liquidation is brought up, most boards refuse to discuss it. They know that the company is essentially charged with the purpose of surviving.

It is true that sometimes *partial* suicide is contemplated—in the name of giving the company back to the shareholders. Exxon's managers, during the early 1980s, boosted their share price by spending up to $2.5 billion per year of the company's money, buying back their own shares. They had more money in the kitty than they knew how to invest profitably in their core business. Perhaps the correct analogy is not a suicide attempt but a slow dissipation. And yet Exxon is large and wealthy enough that it can afford such episodes; other companies would find themselves not merely weakened, but imperiled.

It is far more likely that an organization will opt to stay alive even when its purpose disappears. In the United Kingdom, there was a very active antiapartheid organization which held a great meeting after the election of Nelson Mandela to the presidency of South Africa. Clearly, apartheid was no longer a threat. So the organization decided to combat international racism. Anything to keep alive! Most companies seek life with equal passion and zeal.

In itself, however, that argument may not be enough to convince people like the Dutch journalist. A more convincing argument arises when we look at the cost, to society and the rest of us, of letting corporations die prematurely.

## The Price of a Company's Death

Consider what happens when a company dies.

> The community of people bound with that company is torn apart.
>    People lose jobs; they are set adrift, without a work community.
> The debt the company owes to its previous generations, who gave
>    themselves to its future, can no longer be fulfilled.
> And the company's constituents—its customers and suppliers—are
>    bereaved.

This is a particularly acute problem in developing nations, where private companies are often responsible for great portions of a country's infrastructure. In some African countries, Shell supplied as much as one-third of the oil supply. The country's social fabric would disintegrate if we stopped. To be sure, some other company would take over the function, but that would still involve a painfully difficult transition period—particularly if the reasons for Shell's death had nothing to do with its performance in that country. The shock could, in itself, be difficult for the country to recover from.

People do, in fact, mourn when a company dies. A premature death means unnecessary suffering in the environment of the deceased company. A company's demise causes disruptions, loss of values, and moral and physical danger—both to people and to other companies. Witness the mill towns in New England, or the consequences of dying industries in the Midlands in the United Kingdom. In the midst of the Great Depression, 60 years ago, British writer J. B. Priestley formulated the need for continuity in business, as follows in his *English Journey:*

> The industry had to be "rationalized"; and the National Ship-
> builders' Security, Ltd., proceeded to buy up and then close
> down what were known as "redundant" yards. . . . Stockton

and the rest were useless as centers for new enterprises. They were left to rot. And that perhaps would not have mattered very much, for the bricks and mortar of these towns are not sacred, if it were not for one fact. These places left to rot have people living in them. Some of these people are rotting too.

Such people appear to have been overlooked; or perhaps they were mistaken for bits of old apparatus, left to rust and crumble away. . . . You may do a good stroke of work by declaring the Stockton shipyards "redundant," but you cannot pretend that all the men who used to work in those yards are merely "redundant" too. . . . The planning did not take into account the only item that really matters—the people.[6]

This type of community destruction is often described as an inherent problem with capitalism, or as the dark side of multinational companies. But it is actually a phenomenon that takes place whenever living companies decay into mere economic companies and then pass away. If far more companies lived somewhat longer, we would see far fewer such scenes.

A company's premature demise is almost certainly equally damaging to its shareholders. The present-day value of an average 50 years of maximized profits is quite likely to be lower than the present-day value of 200 years of moderate profits combined with an expansion of the company's activities in all the areas for which it is able to develop potential.

James Collins and Jerry Porras found strong evidence for this in their research into "visionary companies":

Visionary companies attain extraordinary *long-term* performance. An investment of $1 in visionary company stock on January 1, 1926, and reinvestment of all dividends, would have grown to $6,356.—. . . over fifteen times the general market.[7]

Consider, in that light, the argument that companies should make their first priority the return on investment to shareholders. Fifteen times *more* shareholder value is available for *not* putting profits first.

A reduction of the corporate mortality rate would seem to be advantageous for all parties: members, suppliers and contractors, the community, and shareholders. If you are a manager, the choice is yours: running a company as a maximizer of profits on the one hand, and existing for 30 or 40 years; or running the company to be professionally good at what it does and to be a good citizen that stays in harmony with a changing world, and creating a legacy that may last decades longer and reward shareholders more in the bargain.

# 11

# Power

## *Nobody Should Have Too Much*

IT IS NOT ONLY THE SCARCITY FACTOR OF CAPITAL THAT HAS changed in the 50 years since the end of the second world war. There is growing evidence that we should give more serious thought to the way power is exercised inside a company. In the immediate postwar years, this was never an issue.

In 1945, my home town, Rotterdam, was left with its heart bombed out, its port systematically destroyed. The memory of the Great Depression was still fresh in the mind. Even my generation, then only in its teens, remembered the breadlines of the 1930s. We remembered the collapse of once-great firms, which left their former employees and laborers behind with damaged self-respect and little hope for the future.

After the euphoria of the Liberation (which in Holland is still written with a capital *L*) came, with the Marshall Plan, a dogged mixture of realism and idealism. There would be social equality to prevent the misery of the crisis years from reemerging. The rebuilding of the town, the port, and the factories would create wealth for a "new beginning" (as we called it) after the depths of the war.

The times created a great feeling of togetherness. Everybody pulled their weight for the general good. If the country did well, if Rotterdam did well, and if our companies did well, we all knew we'd be doing fine. And it worked.

By the early 1950s, there was an atmosphere of enormous hope. Everything could be done—no, it *would* be done. It was great to play on a winning team. At the same time, there was not much wealth. Life was simple and spartan by today's standards. We did not question the necessity of creating material wealth. Anybody could see the need for it. There were constant reminders in the lingering memory of the Great Depression, the war damage, and the displaced persons everywhere. Material wealth was necessary to repair and to prevent it from ever happening again.

Nor did we question what, in retrospect, seems like a paradoxical premise: that the most effective way to produce this wealth was to join together in large institutions. We knew that we could create wealth only on a large scale. To be sure, we had all seen how institutions could become vicious. Nobody was naive about the potential dangers in political parties, states, or armies. At the level of the nation-state, a number of safeguards were built into the political system that still make democracy feasible in Western Europe and Japan today.

The most basic safeguard against having a political system taken over by dictatorial power was a mandate that no existing leaders could override the voters' ability to replace them. As Karl Popper has argued convincingly, it is the ability to oust its leaders without a crisis, more than the right to vote the leaders in, that is key in a democracy. Yet we did not always have that capability at the level below the nation-state. To be sure, we had many institutions with this safeguard: trade unions, political parties, local governments, clubs, and school committees. But in companies, where the employees could not rid themselves of their managers, we did not bother with the pretense of democracy.

It might be that we relied on another democratic safeguard: if we did not like it, we could quit. But my generation did not exploit that basic freedom. When we joined a company, we joined with the premise that we were in it for life. The safeguard of the ability to quit did not seem to matter; it was overwhelmed by our need to produce large amounts of material wealth quickly. We were, in short, still oriented to living in a crisis.

The postwar generation understood that the individual would be ineffective in the face of the massive task ahead. We knew that we could repair the damage done by the war and raise the standard of living only by joining together. United, we would stand. Divided, we would fall. The whole would be more productive than the sum of the parts.

Thus, in those postwar days in the Netherlands, most young members of the workforce set out to join large companies or governmental organizations. Shell, Unilever, and Philips were the favorite choices. They and many other companies like them had existed and survived from the time of our fathers. Surely, they would still exist at the time of our children.

Perhaps there was a risk of abuse of power in these companies all through the 1950s and 1960s. But it would take until 1968 for the weaknesses of most companies' dominant organizational principles, the abuses of their decision-making processes, and the resulting under-utilization of their human resources to be aired in public debate. In the meanwhile, we were content to subordinate ourselves to the overall well-being of the companies, which would raise our standards of living.

We also accepted, unquestioningly, the organizational principles that years of war had shown to be effective: top-level decision making in strongly disciplined hierarchies. Information flowed upward and commands, downward. Planning was centralized. The armies of the Allied nations provided a matchless example for the way business should organize itself. These armies had, in the end, prevailed, hadn't they? Now, the faster growth in material well-being that would result from becoming a member of a large corporation seemed well worth the price of submitting to strong central leadership vested in relatively few people. We cared more about the quantity and distribution of what we would produce than about the manner in which it would be produced.

## An Ethic of Distributed Power

As organized institutions, corporations are older than political parties and trade unions; but they are far younger than the great institutional forces of civilization: the family, the tribe, the kingdom, religion, science, and soldiering.

It's no wonder, therefore, that many organizational principles applied in companies smack strongly of copycatting from their older siblings. The military has been a particularly strong source of inspiration. You can hear it in the continual calls for "strategy." Strategy, in the military, is the act of guiding and steering an army toward victory. Other phrases, such as "top-level decision making" and "centralized planning," also have a romantic attraction that stems, perhaps, from their military heritage. Managers can see themselves as the Marlboro cowboy, riding the corporation like a horse and steering it into the sunset.

But should a CEO try to guide and steer a company as if it were at war? Should a boardroom be compared with Napoleon's tent at Austerlitz? Like all crises, war offers little time for deliberation among the individuals who make up the organization. The war situation demands centralized decision making; it should take very little time for commands to travel from issue to execution. Wartime also separates decision makers from executors. Information travels upward only and is not shared with anyone outside the command line.

How appropriate are these characteristics as descriptions of a business? They may apply to companies in a crisis state, but that hardly represents a company at a well-developed stage of evolution. Although we sometimes describe business competition as a "fight," it is far from the crisis situation of a physical war.

More importantly, the centralization of power is inappropriate for the operation of a living company. It reduces the learning capacity of an organization. The alternative is to develop an ethic of distributed power.

We have seen some examples of distributed power in other sections of this book. Mitsui, as described in Chapter 6, "Managing for Profit or for Longevity," maintained its cohesiveness despite being split into unrelated, smaller organizations after World War II. Even when it came back together, the smaller organizations retained authority over their own decisions. They continued to see themselves, however, as part of the larger Mitsui group, and they made their decisions with the goal of contributing to its vitality.

The issue of power distribution finds an interesting illustration in the Royal Dutch/Shell Group. As noted in Chapter 9, "The Corporate Immune System," the group itself results from a cross-cultural merger—

the 1907 merger between Royal Dutch, a company incorporated in the Netherlands (owning 60 percent of the group's shares) and Shell Transport and Trading, incorporated in the United Kingdom (owning 40 percent).

There are thus two parent companies, one Dutch and one British; they continue to exist today, independent of each other yet interlinked, domiciled in two countries, each with a different legal system. The Dutch system is distinctly continental; it was reshaped during the French occupation in Napoleonic times. The British jurisprudence system, accumulated since Saxon days, has never had the benefit of a good spring cleaning. Consequently, in the corporate laws of these two countries, there are some important differences in the composition and role of corporate boards and their members. The two parent companies must get along well with each other, because there is no court of justice to which they can refer disputes.

The full boards of both companies meet voluntarily once a month, and they call their meetings the "Conference." No legally valid decisions that are binding on both companies can be taken during these meetings. The officers of both companies must hold separate meetings during which they legalize, for each parent company, the decisions at which they have arrived jointly.

From the top of the Shell Group down there is no traditional mechanism to resolve conflict. The group has no CEO. The chairman of the managing directors is only *primus inter pares,* first among peers. One way or another, the members of the Committee of Managing Directors (CMD) and the two boards of directors have to agree among themselves on solutions that are acceptable to all. In practice, there will not always be real unanimity, but there is no good way to force through a decision to which one or more of the members are actively opposed. The minimum that is required is a *quasi-unanimity;* otherwise the decision has to be referred back to the next lower level. Quasi-unanimity does not mean that everybody agrees with the proposal. It means that no one is so violently opposed that he will show a veto card. The chairman has no other power than his persuasion; he has no casting vote or final decision.

In theory, decisions could be forced through shareholders' votes. After all, Royal Dutch owns 60 percent of the group. To the best of my knowledge, however, there is no record of any decision taken by vote at the board or CMD level. This testifies to the wisdom of many generations of directors. To force decisions by majority vote in such a delicate structure, without any legal recourse, would have broken up the marriage long ago. But it withstood the competitive pressures of the 1920s. It withstood the second world war, when Royal Dutch all but disappeared as a working entity during the German occupation of the Netherlands. It even withstood government pressures during the oil boycott in 1973, when Holland was completely cut off by the Arab suppliers and the UK suffered diminished supplies. Had the group's board voted to favor either the UK or the Netherlands with its supply of embargoed oil, the Dutch dominance of the voting power could easily have created serious cracks in the international group unity.

As it happens, most conflicts and tensions do not come directly from the outside world to enter at the board level. Conflicts mostly percolate upward through the system. The coordinators, one level below the CMD level, learn very quickly that it is not propitious for one's career to channel potential conflicts at their level to the CMD. It is far better to reach an amicable settlement with one's colleagues yourself. In their turn, coordinators are not favorably disposed to subordinates who do not solve their own conflicts. And so on further down the line.

Consequently, at many levels down the hierarchy, a lot of people are required to participate in most decisions—and certainly the decisions that will require change. Each person has a quasi-veto power. It is not easy in Shell to exclude people from a decision if they are to be involved in the implementation. After the second world war, this quality was further reinforced by the introduction of a matrix organization. As the popular definition puts it, a matrix is "an organization in which nobody can make any decision on his or her own, but anybody on his own can stop a decision being made."

For all of these reasons, ever since the signing of the merger agreement 90 years ago, the downward pressure on conflict resolution has been a fixture at Shell. Neither internally nor externally is there a desk where the buck stops. The buck stops at thousands of desks, each at its appropriate level. This idea has been expressed as a generic principle: the essential thing about power is that no one have too much of it.

## The Implications of Distributed Power

The arguments *against* distributed power are well known. They represent well-nigh irresistible temptations to many managers.

*It takes forever to make a decision. We do not have that sort of time. The world and the competition are moving forward; we cannot stay behind.* The wide distribution of power can be incredibly frustrating, but it means that the number of minds that are actively engaged in the decision-making process is increased considerably. There is no convincing evidence that it leads to slower action (although it certainly takes longer to come to conclusions). It may well lead to better action, and it may enhance the organization's ability to learn. In fact, there is much circumstantial evidence that institutions are more successful, survive much longer and thrive better if they have effectively given power to minorities to veto or delay majority decisions that go against their interests or better judgment.

*A cohesive decision requires an ultimate seat of power so that the result has unity.* This objection is based on a fallacy. Many managers assume that the crucial point of a decision is the moment when the chief executive has a brilliant thought or has been convinced by somebody else's brilliant thought.

But that moment of conclusion is only incidental to the real impact of the decision—the way it is implemented. In the world of business, only action counts. In other words, implementation is an integral part of the decision and not something separate which happens afterwards. When a decision is made, leaving out the people whose cooperation is necessary may speed up the moment of arriving at a new conclusion, but it will royally lose any time so gained through a slow and almost certainly unintelligent implementation.

*You cannot oblige people to produce results except through authority.* In the end, the lure of power—the need to be wanted and the need to feel in control—deters many senior executives from approving the distribution of power, thus diminishing the institutional learning capacity.

Top managers will typically phrase their qualms in terms like, "I want to sleep well at night." This is only possible, they seem to feel, if they have some sort of certainty. Nothing unexpected and unwelcome can happen in the company unless they can know about it and prevent it first. Or they may feel that the need to "maintain cohesion in the company" requires an "open path" (a controlling path) from the top. How else can the chief executive take the responsibility for the ultimate result of the company?

The usual resolution of this dilemma between control and freedom is, once again, to err on the side of caution—to create a wide-open path of delegation all the way to and from the top of the hierarchy. This tendency plays into the hands of the employees who, at any given moment, do not feel capable of dealing with a business situation. They send their problems and conflicts to the next-higher level of authority. This phenomenon is the obscure shadow side of the more famous delegation-of-authority problem. Game playing, incompetence, or laziness at the lower levels meets the bosses' desire to control, their pride at being asked questions, or the illusion that only senior managers know the answer.

If both the lower and the higher levels in the hierarchy give in to this temptation, the end result is that fewer people with fewer factual knowledge participate in decision making. Once again, corporate learning suffers.

## Upward Impediments

As I noted earlier, relinquishing control can be very frightening. It goes against managers' personalities, their training, and the incentives that they have received all their lives. Now, as I suggested in Chapter 8, "The Tolerant Company," they must balance control and tolerance in a different way. Rather than "steering," they must set a context. "Go ahead," they must say to their subordinates. "You are free to fail within the context of the learning that we have done together. I will watch."

Even when managers accept the idea that power must be distributed, many managers have little experience with the realities. They don't know how to ensure that distribution of power will actually take place.

There is a widespread illusion, for instance, that one can distribute power in a company, and engage more brains, simply by delegating authority. It does not matter whether you simply tell your subordinates to "get on with it" or give them statutory powers to spend money with back reference. If you give them legal power to make decisions, they will make the decisions—or so people believe.

Some employees will be happy to make decisions. Some are eager to make decisions that are not theirs to make. But a top manager cannot count on decisions being made consistently at the lowest level where they should be made, unless impediments are created against upward delegation of difficulties and conflicts.

In other words, make it difficult to move conflict up the hierarchy. Set in motion policies implicitly or explicitly stating that people can ask the next-higher levels for advice but cannot ask them to make decisions. This policy is counterintuitive to many top managers. It flies in the face of their misguided belief that they are a *paterfamilias* put in place to "solve the difficulties of the family and smooth the path for the children."

I learned about designing upward impediments as an operating company manager in Brazil. In Latin America, the prevailing model of corporate culture is the family. The father is, indeed, the *paterfamilias* of the family, the ultimate power and wisdom. Therefore, the weaker members of the family are conditioned to go and cry at "pater's" knees. Things are rarely done without the superior's agreement. And because Brazilians love to play that role, it became very difficult to delegate authority. The senior managers of the company found themselves bedeviled with trivia, but unwilling to give up the burden.

We tried unsuccessfully for a long time to deal with this problem. Finally, we set arbitrary levels of decision-making scale. If a decision exceeded a certain number of *cruzeiros* worth of oil sales, or a certain level of personnel management, we allowed it to be delegated upward to the central office. We chose the levels based on a ratio of roughly 90 percent to 10 percent. In other words, only one-tenth of the problems should be kicked up to the central office. Then we made sure that the central office did not have the resources to deal with more problems than those, so that anyone who sent up more than one-tenth of their problems would have to wait an inordinately long time for results. We also made sure that the local offices *did* have the resources to deal with their 90 percent of the problems. We redistributed people back from the central office in Rio de Janeiro to the field offices around the rest of Brazil, making sure that they were given better titles and salaries in the process. This was counterintuitive; in the past, promotions had nearly always meant a move to the central headquarters. We supplemented these promotions with in-depth training so that local managers would gain the same experience, or more, with such important skills as cash flow management.

There were immediate consequences. Within one year, Shell Brazil's profit jumped 60 percent and stayed at the higher level. But the long-term consequences were more significant still. When the country fell into economic difficulties, the working capital situation in the company began to totter. Other oil companies found themselves stultified and torpedoed by changing credit terms for their supplies. But Shell Brazil adapted with enormous flexibility and speed. Back at the central office, we needed only a small team; people at local offices had all the power they needed to deal effectively with the situation.

## The Living Company Needs New Governance

In Chapter 10, "Conservatism in Financing," I argued that shareholders should give up their ultimate powers over the life and death of companies, because it optimizes the wrong production factor—capital—to the detriment of the shareholders themselves. In this chapter, I examined incidental but growing evidence that management should similarly relinquish some of its own power. If management gives in to the irresistible temptation to concentrate that power at the top, too few brains are engaged in institutional learning.

Where, then, should power be seated in the knowledge-creating company of tomorrow, and to whom should it be distributed?

When phrased this way, the question of corporate governance becomes reminiscent of the debate that took place in the Western world at the time of the French Revolution and the subsequent conceptualization of the U.S. Constitution. It was the era of the decline of absolute monarchy and the evolution of the democratic form of government. I believe that we would find a great deal of inspiration for the forms that corporate governance should take by returning to the debate that took place when we developed the governance structure of our Western nation-states.

The developers of the U.S. Constitution, for instance, are well known for setting out to devise a system that would provide continuity without the need for the absolute powers of monarchy. At the same time, in the emerging nation-states of Europe, people had become painfully aware of the dangers for society as a whole of power concentrated too highly. The results were declarations of basic principles and rights, and constructs like the *Trias Politica* (the separation of legislative, executive, and judicial power and its distribution over three independent power centers, with checks and balances to prevent the one from overtaking the others). Ever since, these three powers have been tugging and pulling in an ever-shifting balance.

Various nations may differ in the exact nature of their distribution of rights, principles, and power. For example, the United States concentrates more power in the hands of its chief executive than would be possible in the Scandinavian countries. And no one is ever completely happy with the distribution of power in their own particular democracy—that is, as Winston Churchill pointed out, until they consider the alternatives.[1] But the basic concept of continuity without absolute power has become a common touchstone for all developed nations. In a system of distributed power, there are safeguards to ensure that no one interest will prevail. In a system of governance based on checks and balances, there are ways to get rid of the bad leader without plunging the community into a crisis.

We need a similar touchstone for corporations. We need a system of corporate governance that provides continuity, with all the requirements that nurture a living company and a human community, without absolute power concentrated in the hands of either shareholders or management.

To develop this system of corporate governance in our age of knowledge, we need to open the debate about power and governance. As matters stand today, companies may too easily suffer the consequences of ultimate power given to one basic interest group, the shareholders, whereas the governance structure gives ample opportunity to an almost medieval exercise of absolute power by management.

It is no wonder that, under these conditions, companies can become fiefdoms for the few, to be exploited like a machine. Under these conditions, no living company will be able to thrive, if its success depends on freedom, space, and mutual trust between members.

And the role of commercial institutions is an important one: to provide mankind with the material goods necessary for a decent living. More than ever, success in this undertaking is dependent on the extent to which these companies will be able to create knowledge, not in the head of the individual, but knowledge on which the company as a whole can act. This is blindingly clear in the brain-rich, asset-poor institutions that have shown such spectacular growth over the last 20 to 30 years: the law firms, auditor partnerships, software companies, and organizations like VISA. But even the old types of asset-rich company, such as oil and steel firms, nowadays need much more knowledge embedded in their actions than was the case some 20 years ago.

The Baron de Montesquieu, in writing about the principle of the *Trias Politica,* pointed out that separated and distributed power meant "freedom." The inverse—concentrated power in one hand—meant, he wrote, that "All was lost."

Concentrated power means no freedom. No freedom means little knowledge creation and, worse, little knowledge propagation. No propagation means little institutional learning and, thus, no effective action if the world changes. One of the main driving forces of a company is the development of its potential. Can we create a form of governance that maximizes the potential of our membership and thereby reduce the corporate mortality rate? Or is all of that potential lost?

# Epilogue

# The Company of the Future

In a world that is shrinking politically, the world of individual businesses is paradoxically growing. In the global village, the temptation is great to move out of one's regional or national niche into a wider and therefore more unfamiliar environment. Even those companies that resist the temptation run the risk that the outside world will invade their home turf.

Over time, as a result, fewer and fewer companies will live and work in an environment over which they have a lot of control. More and more companies will be growing potatoes in the Andes, as it were, rather than in a glass house. With their habitat shrinking, economic companies might become an endangered species—pushed back into isolated, small niches and legally protected national parks.

In short, in the global village, the economic companies risk being the economic losers. The shrinking world will need more and more living companies.

What, then, does a healthy company of the future look like? How do we recognize when we are on the right track toward a healthy living company? And if a company does not look very healthy, what could the concerned manager do to restore it?

A healthy living company will have members, both humans and other institutions, who subscribe to a set of common values and who believe that the goals of the company allow them and help them to achieve their own individual goals. Both the company and its constituent members have basic driving forces: they want to survive, and once the conditions for survival exist, they want to reach and expand their potential. The underlying contract between the company and its members (both individuals and other institutions) is that the members will be helped to reach their potential. It is understood that this, at the same time, is in the company's self-interest. The self-interest of the company stems from its understanding that the members' potential helps create the corporate potential.

The nature of this underlying contract creates trust, which results in levels of productivity that cannot be emulated by discipline and hierarchical control. Trust also allows space and tolerance both inside the hierarchy and toward the outside world. These are basic conditions for the high levels of institutional learning that will, on occasion, be very necessary.

The company has a will; thus, it makes choices. As a result of making choices, it may diverge from the conditions or the values in its environment. Continued disharmony with its world will lead to a crisis and may be mortal.

To avoid a crisis and to perceive a diverging environment, the company must be open to the outside world. Openness to the outside world means that there is tolerance for entry of new individuals and ideas. However, members know "who is us" and "who is not us."

The membership of the community is variable, not only through the individuals who enter and leave over time, but also by enlargement or reduction of the whole over time.

Sometimes, members are forced out or converted into supplier or contractor status (which is a money relationship)—as when their value system is not harmonious with the company's value system. This shift is healthy for the institution, because harmonized value systems are a basic requirement for corporate cohesion. Sometimes, reduction in membership takes place, because an inner group of members redefines "who is us" and enlarges the definition of "who is not us." This may not be healthy, because of the shock to the trust levels of the remaining members.

The human members of a healthy company are mobile, both in the different jobs they perform during their careers and in the places where they perform those jobs. They network, they meet, and they communicate across the whole organization. There is mutual trust that people will act fairly, and the leaders are as honest as one can expect from human beings. People know their trade. Power is distributed; there are checks and balances in the power system, and the present leaders understand that they are but one generation out of many still to come.

Besides members, the company will have physical (capital) assets, which the company uses for one or several economic activities to earn a living. Once survival is assured, the economic activity is used as the basis from which the community develops its potential.

While it is engaged in a particular activity at a particular place, the work community is surrounded by suppliers (of materials, of capital, of human labor and intelligence), by customers, by the regional or national community, and by other stakeholders who are all part of its world and with whom it must maintain a state of harmony.

If survival is at stake, the community will scuttle assets and try to change the content or nature of its economic activity before it scuttles people.

Everything the company does is rooted in the two main hypotheses of this book:

1. The company is a living being.
2. The decisions for action made by this living being result from a learning process.

In setting out these characteristics, I have tried to portray not just the economic aspects of a living company, but the psychological, sociological, and anthropological aspects. All of these aspects complement, rather than fight, each other. The relevance of these aspects was already foreshadowed in the definition of a living company from the Prologue of this book: "[A living company is] financially conservative with a staff that identifies with the company and a management that is tolerant and

sensitive to the world in which they live." Both descriptions make clear
that the priorities of the management of a living company cannot be
exclusively expressed in economic terms.

If corporate health falters, the priority should be on mobilizing the
maximum human potential, on restoring or maintaining trust and civic
behavior, and on increasing professionalism and good citizenship.

Everything starts there. If companies can meet those conditions, I
believe that average corporate life expectancy will begin to rise, to meet
its potential span; and all of humanity will benefit as a result.

This is not to say that companies should live forever. In the corporate species, however, the gap between average and maximum life
expectancy is still so wide that it may be concluded that too many companies suffer an untimely death. A reduction of the corporate mortality rate would seem to be advantageous for all parties: members, suppliers and contractors, the community, and shareholders.

# Notes

### PROLOGUE

### The Lifespan of a Company

1. Royal Dutch/Shell Group Planning PL/1, *Corporate Change: A Look at How Long-Established Companies Change,* September 1983. This private study is not available to the public; I have quoted extensively from it in this book, however. The facts and figures on the first two pages of this chapter are all taken from this study. In all, 30 companies were studied, for 27 of which case histories were prepared. The companies were Anglo American Corporation, Booker McConnell, British American Tobacco, Daimaru, DuPont, East India Companies, Anthony Gibbs, W. R. Grace, Hudson's Bay Company, IBM, Kennecott, Kodak, Kounoike, 3-M, Mitsubishi, Mitsui, Pilkington, Rolls Royce, Rubber Culture, SKF, Siemens, Société Générale, Suez Canal Company, Sumitomo, Suzuki, Unilever, and Vestey.
2. Ellen de Rooij, A brief desk research study into the average life expectancy of companies in a number of countries, Stratix Consulting Group, Amsterdam, August 1996.
3. *Corporate Change,* Appendix V, 25.
4. James C. Collins and Jerry I. Porras, *Built to Last: Successful Habits of Visionary Companies* (New York: HarperCollins, 1994), 9.

### CHAPTER 1

### The Shift from Capitalism to a Knowledge Society

1. See, for example, Fernand Braudel, *The Wheels of Commerce,* vol. 2 of *Civilization and Capitalism, 15th–18th Century,* trans. Sian Reynolds (Berkeley: University of California Press, 1992), 466ff; and Henri Pirenne, *Les périodes de l'histoire sociale du capitalisme* (Brussels, 1922).

2. Braudel, *The Wheels of Commerce*, p. 52.

3. The extremes of this world are recounted by Robert L. Heilbroner in *The Worldly Philosophers: The Lives, Times, and Ideas of the Great Economic Thinkers* (New York: Simon & Schuster, 1953, 1986); see Chapter 8, "The World of Thorstein Veblen."

4. See, for example, Peter Drucker, *The New Realities* (New York: Harper & Row, 1989), 178ff; or Ikujiro Nonaka and Hirotaka Takeuchi, *The Knowledge Creating Company* (Oxford: Oxford University Press), 1995.

5. I have taken this definition from one of my old handbooks, by Professor Dr. Wilhelm Röpke, *Die Lehre von der Wirtschaft* (Zurich: Eugen Rentsch Verlag, 1946); see pages 163–172 and 188–200. Different versions of the same definition appear in countless handbooks on economics in many languages.

6. Jean Piaget, *The Psychology of Intelligence* (London: Routledge & Kegan Paul, 1986), 8–9 and 103.

CHAPTER 2

## The Memory of the Future

1. See, for example, Milton Moskowitz, Michael Katz, and Robert Levering, *Everybody's Business: An Almanac* (New York: Harper & Row, 1980), 603–610.

2. *Corporate Change*, 6.

3. *Corporate Change*, 9.

4. Sven Rydberg, *The Great Copper Mountain: The Stora Story* (Hedemora: Gidlunds, 1988), 50. The book was published on the occasion of the 700-year anniversary of the enterprise.

5. David Ingvar, "Memory of the Future: An Essay on the Temporal Organization of Conscious Awareness," *Human Neurobiology* (1985): 127–136.

CHAPTER 3

## Tools for Foresight

1. This story was adapted from one often told by Pierre Wack, who talked of the "Mayor of Dresden." I prefer to use Rotterdam, the city of my birth.

2. *The Independent*, 24 October 1992.

3. Daniel Yergin, *The Prize: The Epic Quest for Oil, Money and Power* (New York: Simon & Schuster, 1991).

4. *The Shorter Oxford English Dictionary* (London: Oxford University Press, 1973).

5. Peter Schwartz, *The Art of the Long View: Planning for the Future in an Uncertain World* (New York: Doubleday/Currency, 1991), 72–90.

6. Art Kleiner, *The Age of Heretics: Heroes, Outlaws, and the Forerunners of Corporate Change* (New York: Doubleday/Currency, 1996), 162–163.

7. Joseph Campbell, *The Hero with a Thousand Faces* (Princeton, NJ: Princeton University Press, 1979), 245–246.

8. Peter Schwartz, *The Art of the Long View: Planning for the Future in an Uncertain World* (New York: Doubleday/Currency, 1991).

9. Kees van der Heijden, *Scenarios: The Art of Strategic Conversation* (New York: Wiley, 1996).

10. Kleiner, *The Age of Heretics*.

11. Pierre Wack, "Scenarios: Uncharted Waters Ahead," *Harvard Business Review*, September–October 1985, 72–89. Reprinted in *Scenarios: The Gentle Art of Reperceiving*, "Strategic Planning in Shell Series No. 1," Shell International Petroleum Company Limited, Group Planning, London, February 1986.

CHAPTER 4

Decision Making as a Learning Activity

1. John Holt, *How Children Fail* and *How Children Learn* (Pitman Publishing Corporation, 1964 and 1967; New York: Penguin Books, 1970).

2. There is a variety of sources available on the cycle of learning, all with somewhat different terminology. The cycle described here is based on Jean Piaget's model of learning and cognitive development. Piaget labeled his phases "Active Egocentricism (Acting), Concrete Phenomenalism (Perceiving), Internalized Reflection (Embedding), and Abstract Constructionism (Concluding)." See Jean Piaget, *Genetic Epistemology* (New York: Columbia University Press, 1970).

The most authoritative source on comparative learning cycle theory is David Kolb, *Experiential Learning (Experience as the Source of Learning and Development)* (Englewood Cliffs, NJ: Prentice-Hall, 1984). Kolb synthesized and expanded on theoretical work by Piaget, American educational philosopher John Dewey, organizational psychology pioneer Kurt Lewin, and others. British management writer Charles Handy adapted the idea of a "learning wheel" for business readers in his book *The Age of Unreason* (London: Century Hutchinson, 1989). It was given practical day-to-day application by Rick Ross, Bryan Smith, and Charlotte Roberts, in "The Wheel of Learning," in Peter Senge, Art Kleiner, Ross Roberts, and Bryan Smith, *The Fifth Discipline Fieldbook* (New York: Doubleday/Currency, 1994), 59.

3. Jean Piaget, *The Psychology of Intelligence* (London: Routledge & Kegan Paul, 1986).

4. This title is influenced by Donald N. Michael, *Learning to Plan, and Planning to Learn* (San Francisco: Jossey-Bass, 1974, 1996). This book, ahead of its time, helped create the understanding that learning has an important place in the life of a company.

5. D. W. Winnicott, *Playing and Reality* (London: Tavistock Publications, 1971; London: Penguin Education, 1980); John Holt, *How Children Learn* (New York: Dell, 1967); Seymour Papert, *Mindstorms: Children, Computers, and Powerful Ideas* (New York: Basic Books, 1980).

6. Schwartz tells this story in *The Art of the Long View*, p. 91.

7. Stella and iThink™ are trademarks, copyright © 1990 High Performance Systems, Inc., Hanover, NH.

8. Some of the first microworlds that led to successful group learning experiments (representing a biotechnology startup firm, the Shell gasoline retailing business in the Netherlands, and the natural gas business after the oil price collapse of 1986) were developed with the help of John Morecroft of London Business School; David Lane, then of Shell International and now at the London School of Economics; David Kreutzer of GKA, Inc. (formerly Gould-Kreutzer Associates); and Jenny Kemeny of Innovation Associates.

   John Morecroft also wrote a groundbreaking article on the role of computer models as maps and microworlds for experimentation and learning. A recent version of that article has appeared under the title "Executive Knowledge, Models and Learning," in John Morecroft and John Sterman, ed., *Modeling for Learning Organisations* (Portland, OR: Productivity Press, 1994).

10. Useful results were also achieved with systems developed by Peter Checkland, Jonathan Rosenhead, and Colin Eden.

11. Peter Senge, Art Kleiner, Charlotte Roberts, Richard Ross, and Bryan Smith, *The Fifth Discipline Fieldbook* (New York: Doubleday/Currency, 1994).

CHAPTER 5

Only Living Beings Learn

1. Since 1974 this attitude toward large corporations has changed somewhat. See "Everybody's Favorite Monster," *The Economist,* March 1993.

2. R. B. McLeod, "Obituary for William Stern," *Psychological Review* 45, no. 5, (September 1938).

3. William Stern, *Person und Sache, Zweiter Band: Die menschliche Persönlichkeit,* 2nd ed. (Leipzig: Verlag von Johann Ambrosius Barth, 1919), 6, 9, and 40ff.

4. Francisco Varela, "Organism: A Meshwork of Selfless Slaves," in *Organism and the Origin of Self,* ed. A. Tauber (Boston: Kluwer Associates, 1991), 79–107.

5. Simon Schama, *The Embarrassment of Riches* (Berkeley: University of California Press, 1988), 334.

6. Ibid., 345.

7. Stern, *Person und Sache,* 55ff: "III. Die Aufnahme der Fremdzwecke in den Selbstzweck (Introzeption)."

CHAPTER 6

Managing for Profit or for Longevity

1. *Corporate Change,* 10. The remark is attributed to Lord Cole, chairman of Unilever.
2. William Stern, *Person und Sache, Zweiter Band: Die menschliche Persönlichkeit,* 2nd ed., "II. Das System der Fremdzwecke (Heterotelie)" (Leipzig: Verlag von Johann Ambrosius Barth, 1919), 49.
3. Robert D. Putnam, *Making Democracy Work: Civic Traditions in Modern Italy* (Princeton, NJ: Princeton University Press, 1993), 165.
4. Joe Jaworski, *Synchronicity: The Inner Path of Leadership* (San Francisco: Berrett-Koehler, 1996), 131ff.

CHAPTER 7

Flocking

1. Jeff S. Wyles, Joseph G. Kimbel, and Allan C. Wilson, "Birds, Behavior and Anatomical Evolution," *Proceedings of the National Academy of Sciences,* July 1993.
2. From an interview with Bram Roza, head of Group Training, Royal Dutch/Shell, in the Dutch language magazine *Shell Venster,* January/February 1994.

CHAPTER 8

The Tolerant Company

1. *Corporate Change,* p. 12.
2. Milton Moskowitz, Robert Levering, and Michael Katz, *Everybody's Business: A Field Guide to the 400 Leading Companies in America* (New York: Doubleday/Currency, 1990), 529.
3. *Corporate Change,* p. 9.
4. For a fuller development of this theme, see Charles Hampden-Turner, *Charting the Corporate Mind* (New York: The Free Press, 1990).
5. Henry Mintzberg, *The Rise and Fall of Strategic Planning* (New York: Free Press, 1994), 98–99 and 119–121.
6. Mintzberg, *The Rise and Fall of Strategic Planning,* 98–99, and *The Nature of Managerial Work* (New York: Harper & Row, 1973).
7. The poet is Antonio Machado.
8. Alison Smith, "Empty Room at the Top—Leeds Permanent's Long Quest for a Chief Executive," *Financial Times,* 5 August 1994, 9.
9. Ibid.

10. Ibid.

11. Rachel Bodle, "Everyone a Rainmaker," *Insight* 8, no. 1 (January–March 1994): 23.

CHAPTER 9

The Corporate Immune System

1. Francisco J. Varela and Antonio Continho, "Somebody Thinks—The Body Thinks: Why and How the Immune System Is Cognitive," in *The Reality Club,* vol. 2, ed. J. Brockman (New York: Phoenix Press, 1988).

2. Michael Porter, "From Competitive Advantage to Corporate Strategy," *Harvard Business Review,* May–June 1987, 43–59; *Economisch-Statistische Berichten,* 11 March 1988.

3. Richard Dawkins, "Universal Parasitism and the Co-evolution of Extended Phenotypes," *Whole Earth Review* (Spring 1989): 90.

4. In the case of ICI, a British chemical company, the demerger of the life science interests to form a new and independent company called Zeneca may well have been partly prompted by a feeling within the pharmaceutical division that the division was contributing more to ICI than it was gaining from its parent.

CHAPTER 10

Conservatism in Financing

1. Richard Onians, "Making Small Fortunes: Success Factors in Starting a Business" (talk at the Royal Society of Arts in London, 11 January 1995); published in *RSA Journal* 143, no. 5459 (May 1995): 22.

2. Ibid., 25.

3. Ibid., 26.

4. James C. Collins and Jerry I. Porras, *Built to Last: Successful Habits of Visionary Companies* (New York: HarperCollins, 1994), 189.

5. Ibid., 8.

6. J. B. Priestley, *English Journey* (London: Mandarin Paperbacks, 1994), 345.

7. Collins and Porras, *Built to Last,* 4.

CHAPTER 11

Power

1. Winston Churchill, speech in the House of Commons of Great Britain, 11 November 1947.

# Index

Accommodation, learning by 59–61, 141, 151
Ackoff, Russell, 8
Acquisitions and mergers, 162–165
  compared with catching the flu, 162–163
  as infections, 163–164
Acting, as a stage of conversation, 59
"Aha!" experience, 54
Angola, 95–96
Argentina, 124
Assimilation, learning by 59–60, 62–63, 151

Baring Venture fund, 172
BASF, 111
Beck, Peter, 46
Behavior, shared by primates and songbirds, 133
Benetton, 123
Berlin Wall, 26
Billiton, 164
BMW, 121
Bodle, Rachel, 157
Booker McConnell, 144, 145
Braudel, Fernand, 16, 17
Brazil, 78-81, 86, 116, 195
  during oil crisis, 78–81
Brazilian miracle, 78
British Airways, 62
British Gas, 177
British Petroleum, 70

Business
  definition of, 18–19
  need for continuity in, 184–185
  Swedish and Chinese translations, xiii

Cadillac, 89
Campbell, Joseph, 49
  description of timeless Adventure, 49–50
Capital, as source of wealth, 16–17
Capitalism, shift to knowledge society from, 15–21
Catholic church, 88, 104
Centralization, 153
  of power, 190
Centralized planning, 190
Chevrolet, 89
Chilean potato, parable of, 148–150
China, 98
Churchill, Winston, 197
Civilization, great institutional forces of, 189
Cohesion, 108, 119, 146
  and diversity, 104–195
Cohesive recruitment, 112
Cohesivity and identity, as corporate longevity factors, 6, 9
Colgate, 8
Collins, James, 8, 15, 115, 175, 176, 185
Collyns, Napier, 46, 74
Committee of Managing Directors (CMD), 51, 191–192
Commodities trading floor, 120

Common values, 106–111
  sharing a set of, 108, 111
Community, 6
Companies
  acting on signals to act with foresight, 30
  being successful by learning effectively, 20
  continuous fundamental changes in inter-
    nal structures of, 27
  ecology of and tolerance, 150–151
  economic company, 100–102, 113, 121,
    125, 128, 178, 183, 185, 199
  facilitating flocking, 138
  four key factors for longevity, 5–7, 9, 34
  importance of money to, 171–172
  lifespan of, 1–12
  as living beings, xi–xii, 10
  long-lived, and values, 108
  as machines, x–xi
  mission statements of, 177
  price of death of, 184–186
  river company, 102–104, 106, 112, 113,
    114, 115, 116, 118–123, 124–128,
    180–181
  as self-perpetuating work communities,
    137
  showing strong territorial tendencies,
    138–139
  threats to health of, 161–162
  and tolerance, 142–158
  two different types, 100–102
  units of as living systems, 89–90
Computer models, problems with, 70–72
Concentrated power, 198
Concluding, as a stage of conversation,
    58–59
Conservatism in financing, 171–186
  as an essential for corporate longevity, 7,
    9, 174
Continuity without absolute power, 198
Control, balancing freedom and, 152–
    153
Conventional learning, problems with,
    61–63
Conversation, four stages of, 58–59
Core businesses, 146
Core competencies, 146, 147
Corporate governance, system of, 197–
    198
Corporate growth, concept of, 178
Corporate immune system, 159–168
Corporate longevity
  and decentralization, 145
  Shell study of, 5–10, 12, 15, 23, 108, 110,
    144, 147, 148, 150, 151, 174, 176
Corporate monoculture, 152
Corporate mortality rate, reduction of,
    185–186

Corporate parasites, cultivating symbiotic re-
    lationships with, 167
Corporate reality, money as expression of,
    178–179
Corporate success
  definition of, 176
  interwoven with longevity, 15
  money as a measure of, 176–178
Corporate symbiosis, 167–168
Corporations
  and anachronistic laws, 181–182
  average life expectancy of, 1, 2, 21
  and conservatism in financing, 147
  existence of parasites in, 166–167
  as failures, 1
  laws governing, and investors, 178–179
  reasons for existence, 11
  Why not let them die?, 181–184
Crises, as only avenue for learning, 30
Customer orientation, 11

Dawkins, Richard, 165–166, 167
Decentralization, 144, 145, 152, 153
  as corporate longevity factor, 6–7, 9, 144
  and empowerment, 140
  and tolerance, 144–148
Decision making
  activity in meetings, 57–59
  business versus military, 190
  and learning, as separate activities, 56–57
  as a learning activity, 55–74
  play not considered as vehicle for learning,
    65
  the reality of, 57–59
  in strongly disciplined hierarchies, 189
Democracy, key safeguard in, 188
de Montesquieu, Baron, 198
de Rooij, Ellen, 2
Deutsche Bank, 111
Deutsche Shell, 104, 146
Dilemma of freedom and innovation,
    139–141
Distributed power, 190, 198
  arguments against, 193
  an ethic of, 189–192
  implications of, 193–194
  system of, 197
Diversification, 144, 145
  by dictum, 147
  during the 1970s, 146, 164
  by tolerance, 147
Diversity, 145, 146, 151
  and cohesion, 104–105
Downsizing, and corporate health, 161
DuPont, 5, 23, 145
Du Pont, Pierre S., IV, 24
DYNAMO, 68

E&P (exploration and production),
    32–33
Ecology, 129–168
    as distinction of living company, 24
    in organizations, 131
Economic companies, 100–102, 113, 121,
    125, 128, 178, 183, 185, 199
    definition of, 19, 21
    under today's legislation, 179–180
Economic success versus learning, 18–20
*Economist*, 47
Einstein, xiii
Embedding, as a stage of conversation, 58
Employee assessment, by teams, 117
Empowerment and decentralization, 140
Environment, definition of, 26
Ethiopia, 96–97
Evolution, 169–198
    definition of, 171
    as distinction of living company, 24
    money as governor of, 174–175
Executives, salaries of, 107
Exit rules, 124–125
Exxon, 11, 127, 183

Financial-based planning, 42–43
Financial conservatism, as corporate
    longevity factor, 7, 9, 174
*Financial Times,* 19, 155, 156
Financing
    acting as governor, 173
    conservatism in, 171–186
Fisher-Price, 64
Flocking, 131–141
    behavior of titmouse, 134–135
    in organizations, 135–137
Ford, 8
Ford Escort, 121
Foresight, tools for, 38–54
Forrester, Jay, 68–69, 72
*Fortune,* 19
Freedom, balancing control and, 152–153,
    194
French Revolution, 196
Future
    dealing with, 38–54
    memories of, 22–37, 41, 42, 48
    predicting the, 39

General Monty, 95–96
General Motors, 7, 8, 11, 23, 24, 89,
    91
Genetic clock, 131–133
Great Depression of the 1930s, 17, 39, 184,
    188
Groupthink, 113
Gulf War of 1991, 65

Hanover Insurance Company, 71
Hawken, Paul, 148
Hewlett-Packard, 175
Hoechst, 111
Holt, John, 55, 63–64
*Homo economicus,* 82, 85–86, 176
Hudson Bay Company, 5
Hudson Institute, 45
Human capital, 137
Human contract, and trust, 118–122
Human potential, developing, 117–118

IBM, 7, 11
Identity
    boundaries of, 103
    sense of, 8
I. G. Farben, 111
Implicit contract, and river company,
    118–122, 125
Ingvar, David, 34–37, 38, 41, 59
Innovation
    as behavior shared by primates and song-
        birds, 133, 134
    and the dilemma of freedom, 139–141
Institutional learning, 139
Interactions between entity and world, three
    types of, 91–92
Intergenerational learning, 133
Introception, 90–93, 94, 103
    as key function of the persona of complex
        entities, 92
Investors, and corporation laws, 178–179

Jaworski, Joe, 122
Job mobility, 137

Kahn, Herman, 44–45, 46, 53
Kenya, 116
Kleiner, Art, 47, 63
Knowledge society, shift from capitalism to,
    15–21
Kodak, 5

Labor
    as a commodity, 17
    as source of wealth, 16–17
Land and natural resources, as source of
    wealth, 16–17
Leaders, and learning, 56
Learning, 13–74
    by accommodation, 59–61, 141, 151
    by assimilation, 59–60, 62–63, 151
    as basis for success, 20–21
    changes within companies as aspect of, 27
    and decision making, as separate activities,
        56–57
    as discovery through play, 64

Learning *(continued)*
  as distinction of living company, 24
  versus economic success, 18–20
  to play, 63–66
  problems with conventional approach to,
    59–63
  ways companies traditionally accomplish,
    61–63
Learning company definition, 21
Leeds, 156
Legislation, necessity for new, 181–182
Lego, 64
Living beings
  persona of, 81–86
  as prerequisite for learning, 77-99
Living companies, 155, 178, 183, 185
  defining, 9–12
  and discipline, 119
  four distinctions of, 24
  future for, 199–202
  and implicit membership contract, 119
  members of, 201
  needing new governance, 196–198
  and raiders, 180
  under today's legislation, 180–182
  and tolerance, 159
Lockheed Aircraft, "skunkworks" of, 135,
  147
LOGO, 67, 73

Machado, 155, 157
MacLeod, R. B., 84
Management
  changed by good scenarios, 46
  as a learning process, 157
  by objectives, 43
  relinquishing some power, 196
  and ship metaphor, 154–155
  steering as art of, 154
  of tolerance, 153–158
Managerial science, 82
Managers
  of capital assets, 127
  failed perceptions of, five different theories
    for, 28–37
  supply of 112–113, 115
  Theory 1, managers are stupid, 28–29
  Theory 2, seeing only when crisis opens
    eyes, 29–31
  Theory 3, seeing only what is already ex-
    perienced, 31–32
  Theory 4, not seeing what is emotionally
    difficult to see, 32–34
  Theory 5, seeing only what is relevant to
    personal view of future, 34–37
Manager-shareholder relationship, 181
Managing for profit or longevity, 100–128

Mandela, Nelson, 183
Marketing companies, and nationalization,
  124
Marshall Plan, 187
Maslow, Abraham, 118
Matrix organization, 192
Mayor of Rotterdam parable, 38–39
McCutcheon, Ian, 21
McMaster, Michael, 92
McNamara, Robert S., 154
Meiji Restoration, 110
Memories of the future, 22–37, 41, 42, 48
Mergers and acquisitions, 162–165
  compared with catching the flu, 162–
    163
  as infections, 163–164
Military, and job mobility, 137
Mintzberg, Henry, 153, 154
Mission statements, 177
MIT Media Lab, 64
Mitsubishi Sjohi, 110
Mitsui, 108–111, 145, 190
Mitsui Bussan, 110–111
Mitsui Petro Chemical, 111
Mitsui, Takatoshi, rules and guidelines of,
  109
Mitsui Zaibatsu, 111
Mobility, 136
  as behavior shared by primates and song-
    birds, 133, 134
  and social transmission, as criteria for
    learning, 135
Mobil Oil, 81, 96
Money
  as expression of corporate reality,
    178–179
  as the governor of evolution, 174–175
  importance to a company, 171–172
  as a measure of corporate success,
    176–178
  and parasitic behavior, 167–168
Monocropping, 149–150
Motorola, 8, 147
Mr. Z, 105–106
Multinational companies, and mutual trust,
  120
Murdoch, Rupert, 40
Mutual trust, and multinational companies,
  120

Nationalization, and marketing companies,
  124
National Shipbuilders' Security, Ltd.,
  184–185
Netherlands, in postwar days, 188–189
New England mill towns, 184
Newland, Ted, 46, 51, 53

Oil supply chain, model of, 67
Onians, Dick, 172–172
OPEC, 29, 32, 44
Organizational space, 139–140
Organizations
  as a community of humans, 3
  flocking in, 135
Outside world, meeting the changing pressures of, 26–28
Outsiders, 122–124

Pan American Airways, 144
Papert, Seymour, 64, 67, 73
Parasites, 165–167
  and symbiotic intruder, difference between, 165–166
People, development of, 114–117
Perceiving, as a stage of conversation, 58
Persona (identity), 75–128, 180, 183
  as distinction of living company, 24
  key characteristics of, 84–85
  of a living being, 81–86
  not matching the world, 93–98
  as role model, 97
Personalismus, 83, 84
Petrobras, 78–79, 89
Philips Electronics, 7, 189
Piaget, Jean, 20, 59, 60, 62, 67, 83, 141
Pirenne, Henri, 16
Planning and the illusion of certainty, 41–44
Play, definition of, 64
Playing to learn, 63–66
Popper, Karl, 188
Porras, Jerry, 8, 15, 115, 175, 176, 185
Porter, Michael, 163
Power, 187–198
Priestley, J. B., 184–185
Procter & Gamble, 8, 11
Profitability, as symptom of corporate health, 7
Profits, as primary goal of companies, 15
Putnam, Robert, 119

Raiffeisen banks, 104
Rand Corporation, 44
Recruitment policies, 112
Red robins, failure to flock, 134
Return on investment (ROI), 100, 101, 102
Richmond, Barry, 68
Riemon Soga, 2
River companies, 102–104, 106, 112, 113, 114, 115, 116, 119, 120, 121, 122, 124–125
  changing course, 125–128
  how to demolish, 126
  and implicit contract, 118–122, 125

maturity of, 114
and outsiders, 123
turning into economic companies, 180–181
Roosevelt, Theodore, Jr., 24
Rotterdam, in 1945, 187
Royal Dutch oil company, 164, 191, 192
Royal Dutch/Shell Group of companies, 2, 3, 11, 23, 38, 47, 49, 56, 79, 86, 88, 90, 98, 117, 122, 146, 164, 190. See also Shell Group
  and apartheid, 94–95, 119
  ladder of personae, 88
Russia, 98

Sartre, Jean-Paul, 83
Scenarios
  number of, 48–49
  planning, 44–54
  providing tools, 48
Schama, Simon, 92
Schwartz, Peter, 47, 50, 52, 66–67, 131
Scientific management, 140
Senge, Peter, 71
Sensitivity to environment, as corporate longevity factor, 6, 8, 9, 24
Seven Sisters, 32
Shared knowledge, 158
Shareholder-manager relationship, 181
Shell Angola, 95–96
Shell Brazil, 78–81, 88, 89, 93, 104, 115, 146, 196
Shell Ethiopia, 96–97
Shell Group, 2–6, 8, 19, 20, 34, 43, 45, 48, 50, 51, 52, 53, 54, 61, 65, 67, 69, 70, 73, 74, 82, 97, 104, 105–106, 119, 120, 121, 123, 127, 136, 177, 182, 184, 189, 191, 192
  Committee of Managing Directors (CMD), 51, 191–192
  Pernis refinery of, 84
  Planning Group, 28, 47, 52, 54, 55, 64, 131
  recruiters, 114, 115
  scenario, and energy crises, 53
  scenario planning experience, 44–54
  scenario team, 66, 122, 131–133
  study of corporate longevity, ix, 5–10, 12, 15, 23, 108, 110, 144, 147, 148, 150, 151, 174, 176, 177
Shell Kenya, 66
Shell Transport and Trading, 164, 191
Ship metaphor, 154–155
Social propagation, 135, 138–139
  as behavior shared by primates and songbirds, 133, 134

Social transmission and mobility, as criteria for learning, 135
Soft mapping techniques, 72
Soga, Riemon, 144
Sony, 8
South Africa, 94–95, 97, 119, 183
Steering, as art of management, 154
Stella (iThink), 68, 69
Stern, William, 81, 83–88, 89, 91, 94, 106, 107, 167, 176
  metaphorical ladder of, 87
Stockton, effect of "redundant" shipyards, 184–185
Stora company, 2, 24, 25, 26, 34, 145
Strategic planning, 153, 154
Strategy, 190
  art of, 154
Stratix Group, 2
Success, based on learning, 20–21
Sumitomo, 144–145
Sumitomo Group, 2
Symbiotic intruder, and parasite, difference between, 165–166
Symbiotic relationships, cultivating with corporate parasites, 167
System Dynamics, 68–69

Takeovers, as infection, 180
Tavistock Institute, 64
Team, capabilities of, 77
Tercentenarians Club, 5, 12
3M, 147
Time paths, 34–37, 41
Titmouse behavior and flocking, 134–135
Tolerance
  and companies, 142–158, 159
  as corporate longevity factor, 6–7, 9
  and decentralization, 144–148
  and the ecology of companies, 150–151
  as fundamental part of company's ecological stance, 143
  management of, 153–158
  rosebush analogy of, 142–143, 145
Top-level decision making, 190
Training and development, forms of, 136
Trias Politica, 197, 198
Truman, Harry S, 110
Trust, and human contract, 118–122

Unified Planning Machinery (UPM), 43–44, 45
Unilever, 6, 91, 189
Unitas Multiplex, 87
United Kingdom Midlands, 184
Upward impediments, 194–196
  designing, 195–196
U.S. Constitution, 196–197

Valdez oil spill, 127
van der Heijden, Kees, 52–53
van Wachem, Lo, 4, 5
Varela, Francisco, 87, 90, 159–160
Vietnam War, 154
VISA, 198
Visionary companies, 185

Wack, Pierre, 46, 47, 50, 51, 53, 68
Wal-Mart, 8
Walker, Patrick, 40
War games, 65
Wealth, three key sources of, 16
Weick, Karl, 118
Weimar Republic, 39
Welch, Jack, 117
Wilson, Allan, 131–133, 135
Winnicott, D. W., 64
W. R. Grace, 5, 144, 145

Year 2000 study, 45–46
Yergin, Daniel, 40

Zaibatsu groups, 110
Zenith, 8

# About the Author

ARIE DE GEUS WORKED FOR THE ROYAL DUTCH/SHELL GROUP for 38 years, from 1951 to 1989, on three continents. In 1978 he returned to the United Kingdom to assume regional responsibility for Shell's businesses in Africa and South Asia. In 1981 he headed Group Planning, which did pioneering work in scenario planning, in the nature and decision-making processes of large corporations, and in the management of change. From 1981 to 1988 de Geus was also chairman of the Netherlands-British Chamber of Commerce. The Queen of The Netherlands appointed him an officer in the Order of Oranje-Nassau in 1988. He is a founding member of the Global Business Network.

Since his retirement, he has been head of an Advisory Group to the World Bank from 1990 to 1993, advised many government and private institutions, lectured throughout the world, and accepted appointments as visiting fellow at London Business School and as a board member of both the Centre for Organizational Learning at MIT and the Nijenrode Learning Center in The Netherlands.

Mr. de Geus's publications include an influential article entitled "Planning as Learning" in the *Harvard Business Review* (1988) and a lecture entitled "Companies, What Are They?" published by the Royal Society of Arts, London (1995).